# COMPLEX DECISION PROBLEMS

## An Integrated Strategy for Resolution

**K. J. RADFORD**

Department of Administrative Studies
Atkinson College
York University
Downsview, Ontario

Reston Publishing Company, Reston, Virginia
*A Prentice-Hall Company*

Library of Congress Cataloging in Publication Data

Radford, K    J
    Complex decision problems.

    Includes bibliographical references and index.
    1.  Decision-making.  I.  Title.
HD30.23.R3          658.4'03          76-58344
ISBN 0-87909-171-1

© 1977 by Reston Publishing Company, Inc.
*A Prentice-Hall Company*
Reston, Virginia    22090

10   9   8   7   6   5   4   3   2   1

Printed in the United States of America

# Contents

v

# Foreword

The significance of this important book is found in a passage at the beginning of Chapter Three, which deals with phase one of the decision-making (or policy-making) process. Phase one consists of gathering information, generating options, and assessing preferences. This would, the author points out, be all that is needed for policy making "were it not for the presence of more than one participant."

It is indeed a prime characteristic of policy problems that they have more than one participant. They are not, that is to say, one-person, but many-person situations. It is this simple fact that necessitates phases two and three of the policy-making process, in which the participants first analyze the strategic structure of the many-person situation with which they are faced, and then, in phase three, interact with each other in order jointly to decide upon a policy.

Phases two and three of Radford's scheme thus describe how things are and must be in the real world, where there is interdependency between the actions of different participants pursuing different objectives. Real-world policy decisions, in other words, are "political" (in a wide sense of this word). They are not "rational" in the sense of being chosen as the appropriate means toward some set of objectives. They cannot be, since there is no single set of objectives that is being pursued! Instead, there is an element of conflict (and therefore also of cooperation) between a number of participants, each of whom is pursuing his own objectives. In phase two, the players can prepare themselves by making a proper analysis of the interaction process before

ix

entering it. Phase three is the interaction process itself, where the decision is actually made.

These three phases of the process apply as much to low-level decisions (such as: "How long shall the coffee-break be?" in which the participants are the office chief, the junior clerk, and the typist) as to high-level ones (such as: "Shall the rich countries aid the poor in a new economic order?" in which the industrialized nations, the oil-rich nations and the poorer nations are the major participants). They apply as much to corporate policy problems—such as the location of a new plant—as to issues in public policy—such as the construction of a regional development plan. They apply as much to technical problems —such as the location of an oil pipeline—as to human ones—like the treatment of old people in a hospital; as much to external problems in the realm of foreign policy as to internal ones such as conflicts between the functional divisions of a corporation.

"Political" decision making as analyzed in this book cannot be avoided by appealing to a higher authority in whom the power of unitary decision is thought to be vested. Nor can one evade it by attempting to persuade other players to adopt one's own objectives in place of those that they already have. Different participants inevitably pursue different objectives, even when (as is frequently the case) all are imbued with good will and perceive the situation in the same way. When these conditions are not met, objectives tend to differ even more.

The nonrational, "political" nature of social decision making should be seen not only as inevitable, but also as desirable. It cannot be avoided unless a complete monopoly of power is established in the hands of one player or complete agreement is reached between all players as regards their objectives. Either of these conditions (assuming one or other were possible) would almost certainly be undesirable. We should conclude, therefore, that the process described here is one that we should not only accept, but accept gladly.

Unfortunately, such an attitude of acceptance is not general. The real nature of the political decision process is still too often pushed under the rug. Thus the great contribution of this book is precisely in advising policy makers how to accept and analyze effectively the later, "political" phases of real-world policy making. With few exceptions (adequately referenced in the text), what has been said and written in a helpful vein about policy making has referred exclusively to the first phase—that of information gathering, option generation, and preference assessment. It is here that the immensely useful techniques of operations research, systems analysis, decision theory, cost-benefit analysis, econometric model-building, technological forecasting, and the like have made their contribution. Unfortunately, these techniques have often been presented as techniques for decision making. Their real use, as Radford shows, is in enabling one of the players to assess the situation—including his own and the other players' options and preferences—before entering the process in which a "political" solution is arrived at through interaction between the players.

The remaining bottleneck, and it is devastating, is our lack of understanding of phases two and three of the policymaking process. In many practical situations, the work in these phases consists only of the unrelated efforts of individuals who finally arrive at largely unspoken understandings with each other on a person-to-person basis! Thus the information produced in elaborate preliminary studies often has to be channelled through the head of one person, for instance, a busy senior official, who has perhaps set aside an hour for the assimilation of ten man-years of analysis. At the last minute, the presentation may have to be shortened to twenty minutes. Then the official interacts with representatives of the other participants, often in an atmosphere made tense by pressures of time, and they proceed to arrive at the necessary "political" understanding. It is not surprising that decisions affecting the lives of millions often have outcomes that are less desirable than might have been achieved by a more structured approach to the problem.

The great contribution of this book is to describe and link together three phases of decision making in a manner that builds on and updates Simon's original description of that process. The book is a pioneering effort in a new field. Undoubtedly, much remains to be done to ensure the widespread adoption of the techniques discussed. There is a need for more detailed description of the technical work that would actually equip the reader to practice what this text preaches. In using the analysis of options, each increase in rigor has a payoff in terms of the comprehension of the political problem that is being faced. Particular areas in which a more technical treatment will be beneficial include (1) the dynamic analysis of commitments, time-dependent options, and irreversible moves; (2) the differences and connections between coercive and accommodative tactics in bargaining; (3) the appreciation of the credibility of a sanction as a function of the whole strategic structure; (4) the significance of the idea of stability in understanding how participants jointly arrive at policy decisions; and (5) the kind of sensitivity analysis that needs to be done on conclusions derived from a metagame-analytic model.

I think it is important also to consider at length the relationship between the internal and external features of a policy situation. In practice, any group of policy makers has to consider the internal aspects in terms of the interaction between members of the organizations that are participants. This is at least as important as the external situation in which the participants are involved. There are however, important differences that require special treatment in the internal situation. As with external situations, the approach is not to condemn, but to understand, analyze, and deal effectively with the internal politics of decision making.

Finally, an important area to be explored is that of the use of models of different degrees of complexity in analyzing the strategic structure of a decision or policy problem. Both simple and complex models should be used in decision making and in policy analysis. Simple models are useful in summing up the findings from complex ones and complex models can be used to test out the conclusions from simple ones. In briefing someone who needs to be informed, simple models are often the most useful. On the other hand, complex models should always be accessible in case certain questions are raised during the discussion of the subject.

These are problems that will certainly be explored further in the follow-up to this present path-breaking work. In the process, we may hope that new realism will be introduced into the analysis of policies and into decision making. These are achievements from which the world stands to benefit.

NIGEL HOWARD
Ottawa

# Preface

This is a book about difficult and complex decision problems that arise with increasing frequency in modern society, business, and industry. These worrisome problems are not like those that have been treated successfully in recent times by the methods of operations research and quantitative analysis. They are not primarily concerned with the efficiency of an operation or with the redesign of a production process for minimum cost or maximum profitability. They are, instead, involved with the complex workings of open societal systems. They are concerned with questions such as "Do we need another freeway?"; "Where should we locate our new factory?"; "Can we reach a new working agreement with our labor force?"; and "How do we cope with the increasing government regulation of our activities?"

One of the most pervasive characteristics of a complex decision problem of this nature is the uncertainty experienced by those involved in its resolution. This uncertainty is caused by the ill-structured and ill-defined nature of the problem and by the incompleteness of the information available to those who must deal with it. The uncertainty can be reduced to some extent by gathering more information relevant to the problem, but time and effort available for such activities are usually limited. It is unusual, therefore, for those concerned to reach a complete understanding of such a problem before courses of action for remedying it must be formulated.

Braybrooke and Lindblom proposed a strategy for dealing with uncertainty in such problems in their classic work published in 1963 (A

*Strategy of Decision,* The Free Press). In applying this strategy, the decision maker concentrates on courses of action that are designed to bring about incremental changes from the present situation. The decision maker implements any course of action selected cautiously and reevaluates his decision as soon as information about the effects of his actions is available. Using this strategy, the problem is resolved by a sequence of incremental steps rather than by the implementation of a single, more comprehensive course of action. This strategy and others with similar intent are now standard components of many organizational procedures for dealing with complex decision problems. They do not, however, take explicit account of a second pervasive characteristic of many such problems. There usually exist a number of participants in any one problem, all possibly having different objectives and, therefore, different preferences for a range of alternative future outcomes of the decision process.

The interaction between a number of participants with conflicting interests or objectives has been examined in the theory of games. Recent developments in game theory have provided the basis for a practical procedure for determining which outcomes of a conflict situation might be jointly acceptable to the participants and might, therefore, provide the basis for a stable resolution to a complex problem. There are usually, however, a number of such potentially stable outcomes, some that might be more preferred by one or more of the participants and some more preferred by others. Which of these outcomes is eventually selected by the participants and brought about by their joint actions is usually decided during a process of communication, negotiation, and bargaining between them.

Purely theoretical approaches are not likely to provide a wholly satisfactory method of dealing with complex decision problems. Managers and administrators who encounter such problems often deal with them successfully by using methods that have been developed intuitively as a result of long experience. The purpose of this book is to combine these practical approaches with methodology that has arisen in the behavioral, political, and analytical sciences to produce an integrated strategy for dealing with complex decision problems.

After an introductory chapter on the nature of these problems and another that examines their constituent elements, three phases of the process of resolution are discussed: (a) data gathering and problem perception; (b) interaction between the preferences of the participants that determines the strategic structure of the problem; and (c) communication, negotiation, and bargaining between them. Throughout chapters devoted to each of these phases, techniques and methodology derived from a wide range of approaches are discussed. The three phases are then integrated into a model of the process of resolution that forms the basis for suggestions for organizational procedures for dealing with complex decision problems, which is the subject of the last chapter. Practical examples are discussed at all stages. One case history is dealt with at length to illustrate in retrospect how the model for dealing with complex decision problems might have been applied in practical circumstances.

The work of integrating methods and approaches from several disciplines has not been easy. As always in an interdisciplinary endeavor, the risk exists of pleasing neither those in the various disciplines (for lack of rigor) nor those wishing to use the integrated product (for lack of sufficient explanation). In order to compensate to some extent for both of these deficiencies, a large number of references have been placed in the text. These references are not necessary to an understanding of the argument as it is developed progressively throughout the book. However, those wishing to obtain a deeper understanding of the basic theory and experience on which the proposed methods of dealing with complex decision problems are based would be well advised to consult the references on a second reading of the text.

## ACKNOWLEDGEMENTS

I am deeply indebted to Professor Nigel Howard of the University of Ottawa and to Professor David Braybrooke of Dalhousie University for their help and their participation in a number of discussions during the preparation of this book. Their contribution in these discussions and the challenge presented by their ideas had a major effect on the content as it was developed. I am most indebted also to Dr. Malcolm Dando of the University of Sussex for continuing discussions of the text and also for his reading and perceptive comments on the chapters as they neared completion. Thanks are due also to Lynn Ferguson-Tan for her thorough literature research and to Diane Hammar who typed every word in this book at least once and some of them more than ten times.

Much of the research that forms the basis of parts of this book was supported by grants to the author from the National Research Council of Canada and from the Canada Council. This support is most deeply appreciated.

K. J. RADFORD

# 1

# The Nature of Complex Decision Problems

The essence of decision making is the formulation of alternatives and the subsequent choice between them. The manner in which this choice can be achieved has been studied extensively in the past thirty years and a number of formal procedures have been suggested as a logical approach to decision making.[1, 2] These procedures typically consist of a series of steps, that can be described as follows:

1. gathering of information and preliminary appraisal of the problem;
2. review of goals and objectives that form the background to the decision;
3. construction of a model of the problem situation based on the relationship of the factors and parameters involved;
4. postulation of a number of possible policies or alternative courses of action that may lead to achievement of the goals and objectives;
5. evaluation of the likely effectiveness of the alternatives in achieving the goals and objectives; and
6. selection of one or more of these alternatives for implementation on the basis of a specified criterion of choice.

The basic purpose of such a procedure is to select a course of action from those available that will transform what is judged to be a less desirable situation into a more desirable one that can be attained at some time in the future. Many of the procedures of this type that have been developed in the sciences of operations research and quantitative analysis incorporate mathematical techniques designed to identify an *optimum* course of action under the conditions specified in the model. The idea of an optimum solution is attractive because it is related to the concept of efficiency. This concept is a powerful force in engineering and it was the basis of much of the early development of scientific management.[3] The idea of optimization is appealing also because an optimum solution can be defended as being the best there is. It can therefore be put forward as a uniquely rational method of resolution of a decision problem.

This analytical approach to decision making has been most successful when applied to well-defined problems that occur repeatedly in the day-to-day operations and management of modern organizations.[4] Even decision problems that do not seem at first sight to be amenable to this sort of treatment can sometimes be resolved in this manner, once sufficient information is obtained to allow a clear understanding of the problem.

There is, however, a large class of decision problems encountered today that are not amenable to treatment by a formal analytical procedure incorporating a process of optimization. These problems are complex and often ill-defined. It may not be easy in dealing with a problem of this sort to determine where the cause of the difficulty really lies. In many ways, formulating such a problem and resolving it are one and the same thing, since selection of a particular explanation of the symptoms of the problem often determines the way it is resolved. Because only incomplete information is available, no exhaustive list of potential "solutions" can be drawn up. As more information about the problem is gathered, different alternative courses of action may become apparent. Another better "solution" may always be just around the corner. For this reason, courses of action selected in response to complex decision problems are often tentative and experimental, rather than final solutions.

Problems of this nature usually do not have any well-defined boundaries. The area of investigation often tends to expand and more and more related considerations become involved as the work of formulation and resolution progresses. It may be very difficult to evaluate with certainty how much better the future situation would be if a particular course of action were selected. Different participants in the problem may have conflicting views about what constitutes a desirable future situation and about the effectiveness of a particular course of action in bringing' it about. Furthermore, actions taken in one problem area may have significant effects in other related areas. These effects may not become apparent immediately. The consequences of any course of action may appear in a number of widely separated areas over a considerable period of time. No firm appraisal of results of any course of action can therefore be made over a limited time span.

Complex decision problems of this nature have been called "wicked" in comparison to the "tame" ones that yield to formal analytical treatment.[5, 6] These wicked problems are familiar to senior managers and administrators because they are usually encountered at the planning and policy making levels of organizations and communities. They are not (as one might suspect) peculiar to government departments and those agencies operating in the public sector of the economy. Government and business are becoming increasingly interrelated. Policy makers and planners in private corporations find themselves more and more concerned with decision problems of the diffuse and ill-structured type that many have thought in the past to exist mainly in government agencies, in the communities in which we live, and in organizations concerned with the direction of public affairs.[7]

Complex decision problems that are encountered in modern business and government are of many different types. However, they have a number of characteristics in common that will now be described in more detail as a preliminary to a study of the methods by which they can be treated. Many of these characteristics refer more to the situation in which the problem exists than to the problem itself, although in practical circumstances the two are often so interrelated that it is impossible to deal with each in separate terms. Not all complex problems exhibit these characteristics to the same degree, although those described in the following paragraphs are usually the ones having the greatest bearing on the process of resolution of these problems.

## THE LACK OF COMPLETE INFORMATION

The information available to an individual or organization involved in a complex decision problem is usually incomplete. Much of the most immediately available data may consist only of symptoms of a problem (such as an increase of absenteeism at a factory or an increase of violent crime in a city) rather than a detailed description and identification of all its aspects. The natural procedure in such circumstances is to undertake a program of data collection before embarking on the choice of a course of action. However, the amount of time, money, and effort available for such data gathering activities is often limited. In most cases, it is less than that required to obtain enough relevant information to understand the problem completely.

There are three main effects of this limited availability of information. First, it is generally impossible for anyone involved to construct a comprehensive model of the decision situation that includes all relevant parameters and the relationships between them. No formulation of a complex problem can be assumed automatically to contain all possible solutions to the problem. With only limited information available, those involved may therefore be left with a sense of incompleteness in their understanding of the problem and the feeling that the best solution may elude them.

Second, in situations of limited information, it is not necessarily the case that two different participants in a problem have the same information available to them. In actual fact, the information available to two participants will generally be different, unless there has been complete and continuing communication between them. Each participant's perception of the problem in which he is involved is based on the information available to him and depends on the nature of his motivations, spheres of competence, experience and judgement. The perceptions of a problem by participants are, therefore, incomplete and necessarily subjective, although there is a natural tendency for anyone who has studied a problem to assume that he has the facts and that what he perceives is the real situation.

Third, lack of complete information leads to uncertainty about the exact nature and significance of past events as well as about the possible occurrence of future events and the future actions of others. One major result of this is that the outcome of any course of action selected to resolve the problem may be different from that estimated at the time of decision. Any difference in outcome is due to the dynamic nature of the environment in which the problem exists. It is also affected by the occurrence or non-occurrence of events in the time period between the decision being made and the completion of implementation of the course of action. The longer the time between decision and the end of implementation, the greater is the possibility that conditions will deviate from those that had been predicted. The longer the implementation time, therefore, the greater is the risk to the decision maker of an outcome different from that which had been estimated at the time of the decision.

It is often of little assistance to those involved in a complex problem that a problem of similar nature has been experienced in the past. There may be a wealth of information of a technical nature accumulated from such past experience, but this may be of only limited use in dealing with a new problem. Although two such problems have many characteristics in common, the current situation may have a number of features that are unique and that are of overriding importance. This is often the case in decisions involved in the location of major facilities such as freeways, airports, factories, and power plants. The basic engineering and technical information may be transferable from case to case. However, many important factors such as the impact on the local population and the environment may be widely different from one installation problem to another.

## CONFLICT BETWEEN OBJECTIVES OR INTERESTS

Complex decision problems are often concerned with situations in which a number of objectives must be pursued simultaneously and in which it is necessary to consider all of these objectives in choosing a policy or a course of action. Consider, for example, the problem mentioned earlier of locating a new airport, a new freeway, or a major new industrial facility. The prime objective in such cases may be expressed in terms of improving service to the travelling public or producing a product or a service that is generally agreed to be needed.

In addition to the prime objective, however, a number of other objectives may need to be considered. It may be desired, for example, to minimize the expropriation of valuable farmland, to keep to a minimum any disruption of local communities, or to keep pollution of the surrounding countryside to an acceptable level. Each of these objectives may be met to a greater or lesser extent by any of the available alternative courses of action. It would be rare (although most gratifying) if one alternative provided the greatest degree of achievement of each of the objectives. The more usual situation is that various requirements involve conflicting objectives. In such cases, the adoption of a course of action that allows maximum achievement of one objective may result in less progress toward satisfying some or all of the others. A degree of conflict may arise, therefore, in terms of the need to satisfy all objectives simultaneously.

The task of resolving this conflict between objectives is less formidable when progress toward achievement of each of the objectives can be measured in the same well-understood and acceptable parameter (such as money) and quantitative weightings describing the relative priorities of achieving the various objectives can be agreed upon. However, this is not possible in a wide variety of complex decision problems encountered today. It may be difficult, for example, even to find a universally acceptable measure of the convenience of a freeway to a motorist. Assuming that such a measure can be agreed, it is most unlikely that measures relating to the achievement of other coexisting objectives (such as the minimization of the expropriation of farm land) could be expressed in the same units. There would undoubtedly be further difficulty in finding an agreed quantitative weighting of the relative priority of providing a convenient route for motorists and of preventing the loss of the farmland.

Such difficulties may not arise or may be of minimum importance in situations in private industry in which profit and cost are by far the most important considerations. In such cases, measures of profit and cost can be expressed conveniently in dollars (or some other currency). The contribution or decrease in profit or cost of actions taken to satisfy much less important objectives can often be neglected or expressed in the same terms. However, many corporations are finding that, in today's increasingly complex society, activities that do not relate directly to profit are assuming greater importance. Furthermore, an increasing proportion of the effort of most nations is concerned with activities in which profit is not a major factor and in which measures of achievement of objectives are much less easy to specify.

The temptation in such cases is to try to express the degree of achievement of such objectives in terms of money or of another well-understood measure that can act as a "proxy" for a true assessment of the real benefits and costs.[8] It is tempting also to use arbitrary quantitative weightings to express the relative priority between the various objectives in order to facilitate the decision process. The danger in yielding to such temptation is that important aspects of the decision problem may be overlooked or given insufficient consideration in the desire to arrive at a solution that has the appearance of logical derivation and in which the relative merits of alternatives are expressed in an easily understood numerical form.[9] On the other hand, many feel that, despite the uncertainties, an attempt to quantify parameters is preferable to dismissing the factors concerned as "intangible."[10] In practical circumstances, it is desirable to measure the characteristics of phenomena to the greatest extent possible, bearing in mind the need for accurate representation of the effects and without placing intolerable burdens on those charged with data gathering.

## INTERACTION BETWEEN PARTICIPANTS

In many of the complex decision problems encountered today, more than one participant has the power to influence the choice of a course of action. Each participant can be assumed to have arrived at a subjective estimate of a set of available courses of action and to have a set of preferences between these alternatives. These preferences depend on the participant's own value system and are derived from his consideration of the contribution of the various alternatives to the achievement of his objectives. If the preferences of the participants are similar, it may be possible to arrive at a consensus regarding a course of action after discussion of the problem and possibly achieve some concessions by one or more of the participants. In this case, the choice between alternatives can be made by the participants acting as a single cohesive entity.

However, if the preferences of the participants for alternatives are markedly different, it may be more difficult to arrive at a mutually agreed resolution of the problem. Some possible alternatives and outcomes may be significantly more advantageous for one or more of the participants than for the others. In such circumstances, resolution of the problem can be reached only after a process of interaction between the participants that includes communication, negotiation, and bargaining. The manner in which the problem is finally resolved in such cases usually depends on the relative power of the participants in this interaction.

Decision problems of this sort arise in situations where there are differences of opinion concerning jurisdiction or control over resources or where the activities and tastes of one party impinge upon another's sensitivities or sensibilities. They may occur, for example, when a group of citizens decide to oppose the location of an airport, a freeway, or a factory in an area in which they feel it represents a threat to their interests. They often arise in industrial relations disputes where labor and management are the major participants. It is typical in such cases that neither party obtains its most preferred outcome of the dispute, but that each gains more by coming to a settlement than they might have if the confrontation were prolonged.

## Linkages Between Problems

Complex decision problems seldom exist in isolation. They are usually surrounded by a group of interrelated and coexisting problems.[11] Information that is gathered or symptoms that are observed may relate only to one of these problems. On the other hand, they may relate to two or more areas of current concern. For example, a drop in sales of a product may be due only to a reduction in the disposable income of the members of the population. It may, however, be due in part to a competitive product that has been recently introduced to the market. It may also be relevant in some degree to both problem areas. Furthermore, it may not be clear to the decision maker which problem area is the primary cause of the observed condition or whether there is some linkage between problems to which the observed symptom refers.

Linkages between interrelated problems may have an important effect on the manner in which each can be resolved. This can occur in one or more of the following ways:

- there may be competition between the courses of action proposed to resolve linked problems and competition for the resources necessary to ensure their successful implementation;

- an action taken in one problem may preclude similar action at the same or at a later time in another area, either as a result of lack of the necessary resources or because the reaction to the first move may be such as to make its repetition less beneficial, less desirable, or less acceptable. In the contrary sense, if an action has proved successful in one problem area, this may be considered to be reason for undertaking similar measures in a linked problem;

- if an individual decision maker is involved in more than one problem area simultaneously, his actions and behavior in one area may affect actions and behavior in another or may be interpreted by other participants as likely to bring about some such effect;

- the process of resolution of two or more concurrent decision problems can be coupled, so that concessions by one participant in one problem area can be used to extract concessions favorable to that participant in another area. The formal arrangement of such coupled concessions is sometimes referred to by the term "logrolling."[12]

One form of linking of concurrent problems is in a *horizontal* manner in which problems existing at similar levels in an organization or community (such as unemployment and inflation) are connected in some way. For example, a corporation may be concerned about the increasing degree of regulation instituted by the government with jurisdiction over the natural resources that it recovers and processes. The government for its part may need the expertise of the corporation to exploit the resources, but may feel it necessary to ask for increased royalties in view of the cost of certain other of its programs designed to increase the welfare of the average citizen.

In many such cases, the corporation is anxious to obtain the natural resources that are vital to its present operations, but it has the additional problem that it cannot be sure of the extent of the long-term market for the products produced from these resources. Suppose that an overseas government has just offered the corporation resource material of somewhat lower quality but at more favorable prices and on a shorter term contract than the local government. Both the original parties probably wish to avoid a major confrontation, but both are aware that the other cannot be pushed too far without a major dispute that would be mutually unprofitable.

The situation is complicated by the horizontal linkages between the corporation's problem with its original supplier of resources and its negotiations with the overseas source on the one hand and the linkages between the governments negotiations with the corporation and its problems in funding its other programs on the other hand. Many decision problems encountered in practice involve more complex linkages between many more participants.

Linkages between decision problems may exist also in the *vertical* or hierarchical sense. In such cases, the connections are between problems at different levels of an organization, community or society. The actions of decision makers at one level may be impeded or enhanced by those of others operating at a higher or lower level. Success or failure of a particular course of action at one level may promote or inhibit the use of similar measures at another.

## THE ENVIRONMENT OF A COMPLEX DECISION PROBLEM

Participants in a complex decision problem find themselves in an environment that is made up of social, technological, and natural elements. These elements bear on the feasibility of alternative courses

of action, plans, and policies and affect the preferences of the participants for these alternatives. Each participant has his own perception
of the environment in which he is involved. This perception is derived
from the information available to him regarding the elements of the
environment. The perceptions of two participants of a particular environment may be different, depending on how much information
about it they have in common. Participants may also have perceptions of other participants' perceptions of the environment, and so on
down an endless chain of images.

The environment of a complex decision problem is dynamic rather
than static. This dynamic quality arises first from the interaction of
participants who are in competition for benefits that can be attained
in the environment. It is dynamic also by virtue of the changing
nature of its elements and of the complex interconnections between
them. These latter effects can be thought of as establishing a "field"
(similar to an electromagnetic field), under the influence of which the
interactions between the participants must take place. The complexity
and the multiple character of the causal interconnections between the
elements brings about what has been described as "turbulence" in the
dynamic field in which the participants must operate.[13] The effect of
this turbulence is to increase the degree of uncertainty experienced
by the participants with regard to the nature of the environment and
also concerning the actions of other participants in the decision problem.

## COMMITMENTS IN RESOLVING COMPLEX PROBLEMS

Courses of action required to resolve complex decision problems
often involve commitments that are very costly, if not nearly impossible, to reverse. For example, it would be impossible after having
constructed a runway for a new airport, to move it to another site if
the original choice proved unsatisfactory. Many large projects, once
started, seem to become endowed with a massive inertia that ensures
their continuance despite the collapse of any logical case for them.[14]
Even implementation of measures that are considered to be a limited
response to a complex problem may have substantial consequences.
It is often difficult in such circumstances for those responsible for the
original decision not to become committed to a situation that is prov-
ing unsatisfactory. The tendency in such "limited implementations"
is often to proceed with "improvements" that tend to make the origi-

nal choice more and more irreversible as additional resources are invested in the project.

## SOME OBSERVED APPROACHES TO COMPLEX DECISION PROBLEMS

It is a natural desire of almost everyone involved in the resolution of complex problems that a policy or course of action be selected that is rational or, at least, that will be considered to be rational by outside observers of the situation. However, the nature of complex decision problems (in particular the lack of complete information, the existence of multiple objectives, and of participants with conflicting interests) militates against the possibility of a uniquely rational solution being found in such situations.

Those who have observed the behavior and methods employed by participants in complex decision problems have noted that they use techniques that are apparently matched empirically to the conditions under which the problems have arisen. For example, a common reaction of those faced with lack of information in a complex decision situation is to concentrate on a much simplified model of the problem. This is often preferred to a prolonged and difficult exploration of its less clearly perceptible facets. The reason for this behavior is said to be the belief that "most significant chains of causes and consequences are short and simple" and that much of the information that is available to be gathered is likely to be irrelevant to the problem at hand.[15] The process of simplification allows the situation to be judged on the basis of the factors that the decision maker feels are the most crucial and relevant at the time.

The process of simplification of the data gathering phase is often accompanied by a reduction in the effort devoted to the search for alternative courses of action. This simplification of the decision-making process has been called "satisficing" by Simon.[16] It consists essentially of a method of decision making in which a course of action is sought that is judged "satisfactory" or "good enough." A decision maker who satisfices abandons the principle of optimization and the search for the "best" course of action. He judges courses of action against a criterion of "being satisfactory" in the circumstances as perceived at the time of decision. No attempt is made to find an optimal solution. Those who satisfice operate within the limits of a "bounded rationality," in which choices are made in a simplified model that incorporates the main features of the problem but neglects many of the complexities.

Decision makers have also been observed reacting to lack of information by taking steps to reduce the uncertainty that this lack creates concerning the nature of the problem and the effectiveness of courses of action selected to remedy it. These methods of reducing or avoiding uncertainty include:[17]

- emphasizing short-term decisions rather than long-term ones, thus shortening the time interval between decision and outcome and hopefully decreasing the effects of unforeseen developments;
- instituting an efficient feedback procedure so that plans and decisions can be modified as soon as relevant information is received concerning the conditions surrounding the decision situation;
- emphasizing plans and decisions involving a sequence of steps implemented in such a way that plans can be made self-confirming through the exercise of some method of control.

Behavior of this nature has been confirmed by others working in the field. For example, Argyris has reported a tendency of executives, having made a decision, to marshal human and financial resources in such a way that the future environment is controlled as much as possible. This is done to ensure that the actual outcome is as close as possible to that predicted.[18] In a similar context, Festinger has suggested that a reevaluation of attitudes may occur after a decision, so that a manager or administrator will act to make the outcome of the decision successful even if he has not been in agreement with the original choice of a course of action.[19]

The need for reduction in the uncertainty surrounding the future effect of courses of action selected to resolve a complex decision problem is often the reason for adopting the incremental strategy described by Braybrooke and Lindblom.[20] In applying this strategy, the decision maker rejects the possibility of constructing a comprehensive model of the decision situation and concentrates on courses of action that are designed to bring about only an incremental change in the present circumstances. He selects a course of action that he considers will lead to improvements in the present situation, implements it cautiously, and reevaluates his decision as soon as information about the effects of his actions is available. The reevaluation includes a process by which both the means to achieve objectives and the objectives themselves can be altered if this is judged to be desirable in the light of the new information that has become available. This allows the continuing recognition of alternative future possibilities. It is complementary to an approach recommended by Boulding in which the effects of uncertainty are reduced by a policy of continually keeping open as many options as possible.[21]

The fact that more than one participant may have the power to influence the outcome of a complex decision problem has also been observed to influence the behavior of those encountering such problems. One response to this essentially political aspect of the process of resolution is a greater emphasis on communication between participants. This is undertaken in some cases for the purposes of actual reduction of differences between points of view. In other cases, a participant who has the power to decide a problem unilaterally may engage in a participatory exercise in order to appear to be taking the views of others into account. The emphasis on participation in such activities as urban planning is an example of the recognition of the fact that the outcomes of many decisions in this area depend on the views and preferences of a number of participants. Communication and participation are often regarded as methods of controlling and reducing the effects of the element of conflict contained in complex decision problems.

## Desirable Characteristics of a Method of Treating Complex Decision Problems

Each of the procedures just described has emerged from practical experience as an empirical response to the characteristics of complex decision problems. The most noticeable feature of these procedures (called "strategies and dodges" by Lindblom[22]) is the conscious or unconscious abandonment of methods of decision making involving comprehensive models of the problem and the maximization of some overall measure of benefit.[23] While such model-oriented methods are regarded as useful if conditions permit, they are found to be inappropriate in dealing with most complex decision problems on a practical level. With the abandonment of procedures involving comprehensive models, the desirable goal of uniquely rational choice between alternatives has also been seen to be unachievable. In most observed approaches to complex decision problems, the idea of rationality appears to be related more to the selection of a procedure for decision making than to the actual choice between alternatives as it appears as a step in the analytical model.

This aspect of decision making has been discussed by Diesing in his review of the role of rationality in society and of the many forms that it can take. In dealing with complex problems, he defines a rational decision "structure" (or procedure) as one that "yields adequate decisions for complex situations with some regularity."[24] He maintains that a rational decision procedure must (a) provide for consideration of a plurality of facts, values, norms, and alternative courses of action (he calls this "differentiation") and (b) have the capability of arriving at a unified resolution of the problem based on at least some of the material considered ("unification").

Diesing states that only decision procedures that embody the two characteristics of differentiation and unification "to a considerable degree" will be likely to yield "adequate decisions." The greater the degree to which a decision procedure embodies these characteristics (he says), the more effective the ensuing choice of courses of action is likely to be. In the first place, the greater the variety of information available to the decision maker, the greater will be the range of alternatives considered and the less the chance that an effective method of resolution of a problem situation will be overlooked. Second, the more capable and appropriate the manner in which diverse material is integrated, the more appropriate the means of resolution is likely to be in the eyes of the parties involved.

The characteristics of differentiation and unification are naturally in conflict to some degree. The greater the variety of information that is introduced into consideration to enhance the degree of differentiation, the more difficult is the process of unification and the greater is the task of arriving at an acceptable resolution of the decision problem. On the other hand, the more formal and restricted the process of resolution, the less likely it is that an innovative, creative, and appropriate course of action will be selected.[25] Any procedure suitable for treatment of complex problems must, therefore, be derived from a judicious balancing of these two characteristics.

There are some broad specifications that such a decision procedure should meet in order to be readily acceptable to those with responsibility for the resolution of complex decision problems. These initial specifications can be stated as follows:

- the decision procedure should incorporate the most appropriate characteristics of existing approaches developed in practical experience and in the analytical, behavioral, and political sciences;
- it should be readily understandable by those who may be involved in (or have responsibility for) complex decision problems;

- it should be sufficiently broad and flexible that it can be used appropriately in a wide range of problem situations, in diverse areas of management and administration, and in government, business, and community affairs;
- the decision procedure should be one that can be introduced unobtrusively into an organization, causing a minimum of disruption of existing procedures.

The design of a procedure to meet these specifications and to "provide adequate decisions with some regularity" is the topic addressed in the remainder of this text.

## THE PLAN OF THE BOOK

The discussion starts in Chapter 2 with a detailed examination of the components of a complex decision problem made up of the participants and the environment. Three phases of the decision process are then considered in turn:

*Chapter 3:* the data-gathering phase leading to the generation of alternative future scenarios;

*Chapter 4:* the phase of consideration and analysis of the interaction between the interests of the participants, resulting in the specification of possible future outcomes;

*Chapter 5:* the phase of communication, negotiations, and bargaining during which the choice of a future outcome is made jointly by the participants.

These three phases are combined into models of the decision process in Chapter 6 and the applicability of these models to a case history is discussed. The final chapter is concerned with methods of incorporating a decision-making procedure based on these models into the day-to-day work of an organization.

## SUMMARY

The essence of decision making is the formulation of alternatives and the choice between them. A logical approach to this task (applicable mainly to well-defined problems that are encountered repeatedly) consists of a number of steps. These steps start with information gathering and proceed through evaluation of alternative courses of action to the selection of one of these judged most likely to transform a present, less desirable situation into a future, more desirable one. Analytical procedures for decision making often incorporate mathematical models aimed at finding an optimum solution that can be described as the uniquely rational choice between alternatives.

There is, however, a large class of complex decision problems for which such procedures cannot be used. "Wicked" problems of this sort are usually found at the higher levels of organizations and communities often associated with the functions of planning and policy making in both governmental and business sectors. These complex problems have a number of basic characteristics: (a) the information available to the decision maker is incomplete; (b) the problems involve multiple and conflicting objectives; (c) more than one participant with power to influence the outcome may be involved; (d) many such complex problems may be linked together; (e) the environment in which the problem exists may be dynamic and turbulent; and (f) the resolution of the problem may involve commitments that are very costly and, to a great degree, irreversible.

Decision makers naturally desire to make a rational choice or to make one that will be judged to have been rational in the light of future events. However, it has been observed that those dealing with complex problems consciously or unconsciously abandon approaches involving comprehensive models and the goal of a uniquely optimum solution. Instead, they adopt certain procedures that they consider rational in the face of the complex decision problems that they encounter. These procedures include: (a) simplifying the problem and selecting a course of action that is judged good enough rather than optimal; (b) avoiding uncertainty or taking steps to reduce the effect of uncertainty on the outcome of their decision; (c) concentrating on incremental measures rather than those involving fundamental and large changes; and (d) placing emphasis on communication and participation in an endeavor to reduce the effects of conflicts of interest.

This behavior in effect transfers application of the concept of rationality from the area of choice between alternatives to that of selection of problem-solving procedures. A rational decision procedure must include elements of differentiation (allowing for consideration of a plurality of items of information) and unification (allowing resolution based on an integration of the available information). In specifying a decision procedure suitable for treatment of complex problems, a judicious balance must be struck between these two characteristics. The procedure selected should contain elements of appropriate existing techniques and it should be readily understandable, flexible, and unobtrusive when introduced into an organization.

## DISCUSSION TOPICS

1. Many decision problems encountered in modern organizations are recurrent, and standard methods of reaching a solution can be formulated based on experience in previous encounters with the problem. What types of decision problem are these? Where do they occur in an organization, and what is their importance?

2. Do you think it is possible to devise guidelines for treatment of a complex problem such as the location of a highway or the siting of a factory? What benefits would such an approach bring? Or should each problem of this sort be treated in an ad hoc fashion as it arises?

3. What steps can be taken to relate symptoms of problems detected in an organization with the decision situation or situations to which they relate?

4. How are planning, decision making, and policy formulation related? Are they all much the same thing in different circumstances? If not, what are the differences?

5. Do the activities of planning, decision making, and policy formulation in large corporations differ substantially from similarly-named activities in government organizations?

6. Ackoff has said that "no problem ever exists in complete isolation" (*Redesigning the Future*, Wiley, 1974, p. 21). Do you agree with this? If so, do you agree that no problem can be completely specified? If not, under what conditions can a problem be considered in isolation from its surroundings?

7. Economic rationality is concerned with obtaining maximum benefit for a given cost. Is this a useful definition of rationality in complex decision problems? If not, why not?

8. What effect do human attitudes and behavior have on decision making under conditions of uncertainty and conflict? What is the meaning of rational choice under such conditions?

9. What is the relationship between conflict and cooperation? Are they mutually supporting? Are there any advantages in the existence of conflict in a decision situation?

10. What should the role of the senior manager or administrator be in the resolution of complex problems? How should this role differ

from that of the specialist in analytical, behavioral, or policy matters?

11. What is the role of judgement in the resolution of complex problems? Would it be better to leave these problems to managers and administrators rather than to attempt to devise a broad approach to them?

12. Diesing proposes a "rationality of decision structures." Is this a useful concept and, if so, how can it be applied in the search for a procedure for dealing with complex decision problems?

## REFERENCES

1. Lasswell, H. "The Public Interest." In *The Public Interest,* edited by C. H. Friedrick. New York: Atherton Press, 1962.
2. Eilon, Samuel. "What Is a Decision?" *Management Science* 16 (December 1969): B172–89.
3. Taylor, F. W. *The Principles of Scientific Management.* New York: W. W. Norton & Co., Inc., 1967 (first published in 1911).
4. Wagner, Harvey. *The Principles of Operations Research.* Englewood Cliffs, N.J.: Prentice-Hall, Inc., first edition, 1969.
5. Churchman, C. W. "Wicked Problems," *Management Science* 14, no. 4 (December 1967) B141–42.
6. Rittel, H. W. J., and M. M. Webber. "Dilemmas in a General Theory of Planning." *Policy Sciences* 4 (1973): 167–69.
7. Preston, L. E., and J. E. Post. *Private Management and Public Policy.* Englewood Cliffs, N.J.: Prentice-Hall, Inc., 1975.
8. Hatry, Harry P. "Measuring the Effectiveness of Non-Defense Public Programs." *Operations Research* 18 (Sept.-Oct. 1970) 772–84.
9. Lowi, Theodore. "Decision Making vs. Policy Making: Toward an Antidote for Technocracy." *Public Administration Review* 30 (1970) 314–25.
10. Local Government Operational Research Unit. *Development Plan Evaluation and Robustness.* London, England: Her Majesty's Stationery Office, 1975.
11. Ackoff, Russell L. *Redesigning the Future.* New York: John Wiley & Sons, 1974, p. 21.
12. Tullock, Gordon. "A Simple Algebraic Logrolling Model." *American Economic Review* 60 (June 1970) 419–26.
13. Emery, F. E., and E. L. Trist. "The Causal Texture of Organizational Environments." *Human Relations* 18 (1965): 21–32. Reprinted in *Systems Thinking,* edited by F. E. Emery. Baltimore, Md.: Penguin Books, 1969, pp. 241–57.
14. Rosenhead, Jonathan. "Operational Research in Urban and Social Planning." Presentation to the Second International Research Con-

ference on Operational Research, Stratford on Avon, England, April 1976, organized by the University of Sussex.

15. Simon, Herbert A. *Administrative Behavior.* 2d ed. New York: The Free Press, 1965, pp. 81–83.

16. Ibid., p. xxv.

17. Cyert, R. M., and J. G. March. *A Behavioral Theory of the Firm.* Englewood Cliffs, N.J.: Prentice-Hall, Inc., 1963, pp. 118–20.

18. Argyris, C. "Management Information Systems: The Challenge to Rationality and Emotionality." *Management Science* 17 (Feb. 1971): B279.

19. Festinger, L. *A Theory of Cognitive Dissonance.* Stanford, Calif.: Stanford University Press, 1957.

20. Braybrooke, D., and C. E. Lindblom. *A Strategy of Decision.* New York: The Free Press, 1963, pp. 81–110.

21. Boulding, K. E. "Reflection on Planning: The Value of Uncertainty," *Technology Review,* October-November 1974.

22. Lindblom, C. E. *The Policy Making Process.* Englewood Cliffs, N.J.: Prentice-Hall, Inc., 1968, pp. 24–27.

23. Braybrooke, D., and C. E. Lindblom. op. cit., pp. 21–57.

24. Diesing, Paul. *Reason in Society.* Urbana, Ill.: University of Illinois Press, 1962, p. 178.

25. Bower, Joseph J. "The Role of Conflict in Decision-Making Groups: Some Empirical Results." *Quarterly Journal of Economics* 79 (1965): 263–77.

# 2
# The Components of a Complex Decision Problem

## INTRODUCTION

The components of a complex decision problem fall into two main groups: (a) the participants, being those individuals, groups of individuals, or organizations that are involved in the problem, and (b) the various elements of the environment in which the problem exists. The process of resolution of the problem is concerned with the interaction between the participants and also with the interaction of each of the participants with the environment. The environment of a complex decision problem can therefore be thought of as the arena in which these interactions take place. It is the equivalent of the "action-space" referred to in treatments of other aspects of complex decision problems.[1]

The elements of the environment and the interconnections between them determine the "texture" of the action space in which the problem must be resolved. The characteristics of these elements and interconnections often determine the feasibility or infeasibility of courses of action proposed to resolve the problem. They also have significant effects on the relative preferences of the participants for various proposed courses of action and for the different future situations that they are designed to bring about.

The environment of a complex decision problem is dynamic rather than static. This dynamic quality is brought about by the continually changing characteristics of the elements and of the interconnections between them. The environment of a complex decision problem has been described as "turbulent" in order to characterize the dynamic nature of the interactions between the participants and between them and the various elements of the environment.[2] The dynamic and turbulent nature of the environment has the effect of increasing the uncertainty experienced by the participants, both with regard to the exact nature of conditions surrounding their problem and concerning the actions of the other participants.

The environment has certain elements that are interconnected in a multiplicity of ways and that can be considered under three headings:

1. *social elements,* by which is meant all those matters that are concerned with mutual relations between the participants;

2. *physical, economic, human engineering, and other technological elements* that have a bearing on the technical aspects of a course of action and on the means of implementing it;

3. *natural events* and those events that appear to be of natural origin, but are in fact caused by the actions of others not directly involved in the problem under immediate consideration.

The characteristics of the participants and of these elements of the environment will now be examined in more detail.

## THE PARTICIPANTS IN A
## COMPLEX DECISION PROBLEM

The participants in a decision problem are those who can exert some influence over the outcome, either by choosing and implementing a course of action or by interacting with those who do. The participants may be individuals, groups of individuals, organizations or coalitions of individuals, or organizations. There may be only one participant in a decision situation or there may be very many who are concerned with its resolution and who have an interest in its outcome.

The degree to which any individual, group of individuals, or organization is a participant in the decision process depends on its potential to exert influence on the outcome, rather than on its apparent or open involvement in the problem at any time. Desire to participate in a decision problem is not significant if it is not accompanied by power to influence the outcome, or if it does not lead to the generation or acquisition of the means to exert that power. On the other hand, an individual, organization, or group with potential influence may choose to remain aloof from a decision situation for some time, possibly as a strategy designed to make that influence more significant. The other participants cannot neglect this potential influence on the resolution of the problem in these circumstances. A course of action that they selected while ignoring this one participant might be proven inappropriate at such time as he decides to take part in the decision process.

### Information Sets of Participants

Each participant has available to him a set of information related to the problem or problems in which he is engaged. This information set is made up partly of data and experience that has been accumulated by the individual (or in the case of an organization, by its members) over long periods of time. In part, also, it may consist of information assembled as a direct response to the involvement of the participant in the particular decision problem under consideration. The actual content of the information set of a participant is determined by his experience, judgement, and orientation, and by the resources at his disposal for the collection and assimilation of data. The information sets of two participants are not generally the same. However, two individuals who have had much experience in common and who have remained in close communication with each other will normally have information sets that are much closer in content than those who have been separated in experience and location for some time.

### Value Systems of Participants

Participants in complex decision problems have objectives and expectations that determine in part their preferences between courses of action and the future outcomes that can be expected from their implementation. These preferences are influenced also by the value systems of the participants. Value systems are essentially patterns of belief that govern behavior in choosing between alternatives. Values are the basis of the identification of needs and of the response to needs by individuals and groups. They are also significant factors in setting standards of expectation and in judging the appropriateness of methods of achieving these expectations.

Value systems of individuals, organizations, and groups may appear to be logically derived or they may seem to be disorganized, inconsistent, and unplanned.[3] They may be affected by ideology or they may persist in spite of the efforts of other parties to exert influence on the individual or group concerned. The value system may be deep down and undisplayed or it may be openly and explicitly stated. It may be a well-known characteristic of an individual or it may assert itself suddenly on occasion, much to the apparent surprise of the person involved. Values may be static and unchanging. On the other hand, they may take sudden shifts as a result of some incident, such as the outbreak of violence, a statement by one of the participants, or some natural occurrence. Such shifts can be temporary or permanent, open or subsurface.

While values and patterns of belief are not always apparent or openly expressed, they nonetheless influence the views and actions of those involved in any given decision situation. It is wise, therefore, for every participant to take note of all available information on the values of the others involved with him in a decision problem. In particular, it is important for a participant not to assume that the values and patterns of belief of the other participants are necessarily the same or similar to his own.

Organizations and groups have value systems that in some way reflect those of their members. If the organization or group is tightly knit and cohesive it tends to exhibit the value patterns of its leaders or of a major consensus of its members. On the other hand, if the organization or group is more loosely formed its value system may be much more diffuse than that of an individual. In such circumstances, it may contain a number of different patterns of belief, any one of which may assert itself under particular conditions. Individual members bring their own value systems into organizations and these may have a major effect on the values exhibited by the organization in decision problems in which the interests of the whole group are affected.

Organizations and groups often contain subgroups that hold different views and may have different value systems than the higher level entity of which they are a part. In such cases, it may be difficult to judge whether the views expressed on behalf of the organization or group are truly those representing a consensus arrived at by wide-ranging discussions within it or whether it would be more realistic to regard them as the opinions of one particular faction. Subunits of the larger entity may have sufficiently different views and opinions as to become essentially autonomous participants in their own right. Some writers have suggested that a similar process even takes place within the mind of a single individual, when the many facets of his personality and beliefs are brought into play in the process of making up his mind about an issue.

## SOCIAL ELEMENTS OF THE ENVIRONMENT

The social elements of the environment consist of those factors that bear on or result from relations between the participants. These elements may introduce constraints that affect the feasibility of proposed courses of action or they may act to reduce the effect of other such constraints. Social elements often have a significant effect on the preferences of participants for courses of action and the resultant outcomes.

### The Relative Power of Participants

When there is more than one participant in a decision problem, the process of resolution depends very much on their relative power to influence the choice of a course of action and therefore the outcome. If all participants have roughly the same degree of power, the outcome is often determined by a prolonged process of negotiation and bargaining between them. During the course of these negotiations, the participants communicate among themselves in an endeavor to influence the others to accept an outcome more favorable to themselves. Offers are exchanged and concessions are made, often in return for similar arrangements in related or future decision problems in which the participants concerned are (or will be) engaged together. The relative power of the participants in a particular decision problem often changes during the course of these negotiations. In some cases, the process of resolution is prolonged until one participant emerges in the ascendancy and can use this fact to bring about the outcome he desires.

A participant with significantly greater power than other participants in a decision problem can use this factor to persuade them to accept a course of action that they may have considered originally to be against their best interests. In many cases, the decision by the less powerful participants to accept the proposed course of action is taken because the disadvantages that would accrue from accepting are seen to be less than those involved in a confrontation. The use of power by a participant in a decision situation therefore inevitably involves some degree of coercion. The coercion is often indirect, but it is nonetheless aimed at influencing the thoughts and actions of another participant.[4]

In many decision situations, there may be (or there may appear to be) only one participant with power to influence the outcome. This is particularly so in cases in which governments or large corporations are concerned, and where the opposition to any decision that they might make is weak or disorganized. In such circumstances, resolution of a decision problem can be undertaken as if no other participant exists. However, it is wise for those involved to ensure that no potential participant can acquire the power to contest the decision before committing major amounts of resources to a course of action that might become the center of contention at some later date.

### Widely Held Values and Standards of Behavior

Participants engaged in resolving complex decision problems are expected to act in accordance with what is widely accepted as correct behavior in the circumstances surrounding the problem. Standards of behavior exist explicitly or implicitly in the organizations and communities in which these problems arise. They are usually based on value systems that are generally accepted as appropriate for the group or community as a whole. These generally accepted value systems may be different in some respects from those of the participants in the particular decision problem under consideration.

Courses of action recommended by participants that do not comply with acceptable standards of behavior may be subject to criticism and disapproval. A course of action that is technically feasible and that is desirable in the opinion of one or more participants may come to be regarded as infeasible if it involves a transgression of ethical standards. Generally held values may, therefore, pose constraints on the selection of feasible courses of action in much the same way as the more tangible elements discussed later in this chapter under the heading of technological factors.

### Relationships Between Participants

A participant in a decision problem may have some form of relationship with one or more of the other participants in the same problem.[5] This relationship may be formally expressed, such as in a hierarchical pattern of authority. It may be of a much less formal nature, such as in shared membership of trade associations, professional societies, or even recreational facilities. Relationships between participants provide opportunities for communication and passage of information between them. Organizations and groups also have formal and informal relationships between them that serve similar purposes when two or more are engaged in a complex decision problem.

Since a complex decision problem seldom exists in isolation, participants in one decision situation may find themselves engaged simultaneously in two or more related problem situations. This is frequently the case with large corporations and agencies of government that have a wide-ranging set of activities and responsibilities. Those concerned in two or more problems often establish interrelationships that lead to communication and information transfer across what had previously been regarded as boundaries between the decision situations. Interrelationships of this sort may reveal connections between problems that had not been foreseen and that can form the basis for a more coordinated and connective type of planning and policy making relating a number of problem areas. Although it is likely to be less widely accepted in the sectors of society in which competition is the main motivating force, inter-agency planning is becoming much more common in government and in other bodies that are close to the public sector. The increasing involvement of private corporations in matters of public concern is likely to increase their participation in planning and policy-making activities of this nature. This is most likely to be the case in areas that represent interfaces between the private and public sectors of the economy.[6]

Participants in complex decision problems often seek to establish relationships with others involved in the same decision problem or in one that is interconnected with their own. The most common forms of such relationships are coalitions established to achieve a common purpose and agreements for support of a particular course of action. Coalitions and agreements of this sort are set up with the purpose of obtaining some mutual advantage. They can be stable, lasting over many decision problems, or they may be fleeting and transitory. They usually persist only so long as there is some common objective uniting the members.

### Commitments Resulting from Past Actions and Decisions

Commitments made in the past may represent major constraints on the choice of a new policy or course of action. These commitments may be contractual, they may be concerned with a substantial investment in a previous course of action, or they may derive from statements made in public that can be retracted only at considerable cost in one form or another. If the decision process under consideration is one of a sequence or one of a number of concurrent problems, commitments to other parties may exist as a result of support obtained from them on other issues. Some of these commitments may have no relevance to the problem under immediate consideration. On the other hand, the necessity of honoring the commitments may restrict the courses of action open to the decision maker in the particular problem under review. If the commitments can be renegotiated, the process of redeeming them (or of replacing them with ones more appropriate to present conditions) may have a major effect on the feasibility of certain courses of action in the present problem.

### Laws, Policies, Guidelines, Rules, and Precedents

Every decision problem is considered against a background of laws, policies, guidelines, rules, and precedents that act to some extent as constraints in the choice of courses of action. These background factors may not be explicitly stated and recorded and they may not be applicable directly and solely to the problem at hand. In fact, different participants in a decision situation may have different appreciations of the manner in which policies, laws, and other such factors affect the problem under consideration.

Many policies, guidelines, and rules are based on past experience. Possible courses of action are inevitably assessed with the history of previous activities in mind. Those that represent a significant break with the past are often subjected to a greater degree of scrutiny than actions that are essentially a continuation of previous policies. This behavior is closely related to habit, which "permits conservation of mental effort by withdrawing from the area of conscious thought those aspects of the situation that are repetitive."[7] The counterpart of habit in organizational procedures is the series of policies, guidelines, and rules that are drawn up to provide some basis for standard response to decision problems arising within the organization. Innovators constantly complain about this apparent bias in favor of familiar activities. However, such a bias is probably justified, at least to some extent, arising as it does from an understandable managerial disposition to avoid uncertainty to the greatest extent possible consistent with obtaining a satisfactory outcome.

There is ample evidence that many of the institutions that make major decisions in modern society endorse consistency with the past as a necessary (or at least desirable) characteristic of any proposed new policy or course of action. This seems to be a wise position if the results of past policies and actions have been judged to be satisfactory. There is also justification for consistency of this nature if the problem under consideration has not changed significantly since being dealt with successfully in the past and if the means available for implementing selected policies or actions have not changed markedly. However, when the results of past activities are judged to be less than satisfactory, when new and radically different situations arise or technological or cultural developments occur, there is much more reason to consider taking the risks involved in a break from the past.

There are those who argue that very little is really new and that there is always something to be gained from the study of the history of a problem. They point out, for example, that many of the problems now being encountered in our cities were apparently experienced in strikingly similar form in ancient Rome.[8] The industrial relations disputes centering around the introduction of the computer bear a great deal of resemblance to those sparked by the replacement of human labor by the automatic machine in industries in the nineteenth century. There is some evidence that some persistent problem situations exhibit cycles over long or short periods of time. For example, attempts at a settlement in Northern Ireland seem to proceed according to a cyclical pattern in which similar participants, courses of action, and solutions exist in each round of consideration. Such patterns can be discerned also in repeated reconsiderations of major modern decision problems such as that of traffic congestion in cities.[9] These patterns may provide some clue as to the feasibility and desirability of any proposed course of action.

## PHYSICAL, ECONOMIC, HUMAN ENGINEERING, AND TECHNOLOGICAL ELEMENTS

The range of courses of action that are available to a participant in a decision situation is limited by physical, technological, economic, and human factors that apply to the individuals, organizations, and physical objects that may be involved in its resolution. These constraints may be described briefly as follows:[10]

- *Physical factors*, related to the characteristics of the physical environment in which the decision problem exists. These factors are often concerned with geography, physical resources, climate, and man-made objects. Physical and chemical laws often pose constraints that can be included in this category;

- *Technological factors*, concerned with the state of the art in the development of the elements of technology involved in the decision situation;

- *Economic factors,* including the limits of available economic and financial support for the decision process itself and for implementation of any selected course of action;

- *Human Engineering factors,* concerned with the characteristics of the individuals involved in the various stages of decision making and in the implementation of a selected course of action. These factors may be permanent, such as those referring to physical capabilities of individuals. They may be temporary and may be capable of being overcome by processes such as teaching and learning.

The aggregated effect of these factors is to define limits within which all feasible courses of action in response to the decision situation can be found.

### Means and Instruments of Implementation of a Course of Action

The success of the implementation of a chosen course of action is dependent to a large extent on the individuals and organizations that are to be concerned with carrying it out. The feasibility of any proposed course of action is therefore dependent on the characteristics, strengths, and weaknesses of all the parties involved and on the likely effectiveness of the means of implementation at their disposal. Roles allocated to each should be matched to their capabilities and to their expected behavior under the conditions surrounding the implementation. If the appropriate organizations and instruments for implementation do not exist, or if those available do not appear suitable for carrying out the necessary actions, it may be necessary to create new groups of individuals or organizations as part of the process of resolution of the problem.[11] These groups then become the agents of change in the environment that is affected by the decision and their effectiveness determines the degree of success attained in resolving the problem.

## NATURAL PHENOMENA AND EVENTS

Natural phenomena and events are an important feature of the environment of complex decision problems insomuch as they affect the future state of the world in which the recommended courses of action are implemented. What are often classified as natural phenomena and events are in fact of two different types: (a) truly "natural" events in which there is no discernible involvement by man;

and (b) "quasi-natural" events and phenomena that are a combination of the effects of truly natural forces and the activities of individuals and organizations pursuing their own interests that are not directly related to the decision problem at hand.

Truly natural phenomena and events are familiar to all. Those that take place after a decision has been made may change the degree of effectiveness of the course of action chosen to resolve the problem. For example, a drought or a hurricane may cause a change in the availability and price of a certain foodstuff needed in the implementation of a program of famine relief. A natural disaster involving a new technology such as nuclear power may change attitudes towards that innovation, therefore diminishing its effectiveness and lessening the feasibility of its use in a particular problem area.

Quasi-natural phenomena and events are those that occur due to a combination of natural causes and the actions of others unknown to the participants in the particular decision problem under review. These often arise as the unintended consequences of others acting in their own interest in problem areas that are only indirectly related to those in which the consequences of their actions are felt. If the instigator of the actions could be identified, it would be possible to consider him a participant in the decision problem under consideration. However, many of these actions and their perpetrators remain unknown and only the effects on the decision problem at hand become evident to the participants. Furthermore, it may not be clear whether the effect observed is due to truly "natural" causes or to the actions of unknown persons operating in other areas.

For example, the supply of a particular resource or manufactured item may be an important aspect of the resolution of a decision problem. It may be known that this supply fluctuates from time to time, but the exact reason for this fluctuation may not be apparent. It may be due to large purchases by an individual who needs the item as part of the measures necessary to resolve his own problem, or it may be due to purely natural effects. If the exact cause of the fluctuation or the individual causing it cannot be identified, participants in a decision problem in which it is an important factor have no option other than to regard it as a quasi-natural phenomenon, until such time as its true nature is established.

## PERCEPTIONS OF A PARTICIPANT

The information set available to a participant forms the basis of his appreciation and perception of the problem or problems in which he is involved. This information set is incomplete and is generally different from that of other participants. Depending on the information available to him, a participant may not, for example, be aware of one or more other participants that have the capability of influencing the outcome of his problem. He may, in addition, have a different perception of the elements of the environment of his problem, of the boundaries of its action space, and of its linkages to other problems than do some other participants. The perceptions of the participants are therefore particular to the individuals involved and are subjective. Furthermore, inasmuch as the environment is dynamic and changing, the perceptions of the participants are likely to change as time progresses, in a manner dependent on their individual abilities to gather information about the new state of the environment.

Because each participant's perceptions of the environment and of the characteristics and attitudes of the other participants are based on incomplete and changing information, it is particularly important that the subjective and uncertain perceptions of a participant be checked at every opportunity during the process of resolution of a complex decision problem. The possible consequences of misperception are strikingly illustrated in a study by Stoessinger of the final days before the outbreak of several wars. This study leads to the conviction that the perceptions of the participants were "absolutely crucial," notably the participant's perceptions of (a) his own and his adversary's character; (b) his adversary's intentions; and (c) his own and his adversary's power and capabilities.[12]

Stoessinger found that all participants suffered from distortion of their images of themselves and their adversaries. They tended to see themselves as honorable, virtuous, and pure and the other participants as diabolical and scheming. He concluded that perceptions of power were particularly distorted. In the early stages of a confrontation, participants tended to exaggerate their own power and to underestimate that of their adversaries. At a later point, however, the perceptions often gave way to acute fears of inferiority. In many cases, what appears now to have been pertinent and well-founded information available to the participants was ignored while previously formed perceptions appear to have been practically impervious to change by newly acquired knowledge.

Most complex decision problems encountered in modern business and government do not have the gravity and far-reaching consequences of an outbreak of war. Nevertheless, the lessons to be learned from a study of the greater crises have important applications to the process of resolution of complex decision problems encountered in day-to-day life. These lessons may be summarized by the single exhortation that all steps should be taken to avoid misperceptions both on one's own part and on the part of the other participants in the problem. The manner in which this can be done is discussed in later chapters of this text.

## SUMMARY

The components of a complex decision problem are the participants and the elements of the environment in which they operate. Participants in a decision situation are those who have the power or the potential to influence the outcome. They may be individuals, groups of individuals, organizations, or coalitions of individuals and organizations. In any particular decision problem, there may be one or more than one participant. Each participant has an information set available to him, which consists partly of data accumulated over long periods of time and partly of those data specially gathered with respect to the decision problem at hand. This information set is the basis of the participant's perceptions of the problem. The information sets of two participants engaged in the same problem may be different and their perceptions of the problem may therefore be different.

Participants have value systems that govern their preferences between courses of action that might be proposed to bring about more desirable future situations. The value systems of organizations often reflect those of their members. In some cases, however, subunits of a larger entity may have different views and may become essentially autonomous participants in their own right.

The environment of a decision problem can be thought of in terms of three groups of elements: (a) social elements, concerned with mutual relations between participants; (b) physical, economic, human engineering, and other technological elements; and (c) natural and quasi-natural events. These elements of the environment may impose constraints on the range of courses of action open to the participants and may affect their preferences for them.

Among the social elements of the environment, the relative power of the participants is a major factor affecting the outcome. This relative power often changes during the process of resolution. The process of resolution in cases in which the relative power of the participants is roughly equal may differ from the process in cases where one participant has much greater power than the others to influence the outcome. Accurate assessment of the relative power of the participants is one of the most important aspects of the resolution of a complex decision problem.

Other social elements of the environment include: (a) widely-held values and standards of behavior that may differ from those held and observed by individual participants; (b) relationships among participants in a problem or among those involved in related problems; (c) commitments resulting from past actions and decisions; and (d) laws, policies, guidelines, rules, and precedents. All of these elements may act as determinants of the feasibility of proposed courses of action.

Other constraints on the choice of courses of action may be imposed by physical, economic, human engineering, and other technological elements of the environment. These elements of the environment are factors that determine the effectiveness of the means and instruments of a course of action.

The third category of elements of the environment of a complex decision problem consists of natural phenomena and events. These can be regarded as being of two types: (a) truly natural events in which there is no involvement of man, and (b) quasi-natural events that are the result of a combination of truly natural phenomena and the actions of others pursuing their own interests unknown to the participants in a particular decision problem.

A decision maker's perception of the environment includes a specification of the boundaries of the action space and of the links between that space and those of other concurrent problems. The larger the action space perceived by any decision maker, the more factors and participants are likely to be included, and the more complex the process of resolution is likely to be. The smaller the action space, the less complex is the resolution likely to be, but the greater is the chance that linkages to other problems are substantial.

## DISCUSSION TOPICS

1. Why is the degree to which a party is a participant in a decision situation dependent primarily on his potential to influence the outcome rather than his actual involvement at any time?

2. What are the factors that most influence the preferences of a decision maker for courses of action or outcomes?

3. How can the preferences of a group of individuals or organizations be determined? Can these preferences be related to those of the individual members and, if so, under what conditions can the relation be expected to hold?

4. How do values influence patterns of behavior in individuals, groups, and organizations? Can you give an example of how a change of values has imposed or relaxed a constraint in our society in recent years?

5. Are a decision maker's preferences stable and unchanging or do they vary from occasion to occasion? What factors might cause a change in preferences?

6. Can you give some examples of how values have influenced standards of behavior in recent times? What effect has this had on decision making in your estimation?

7. What are the most important effects of patterns of power and authority on decision making? How is coercion related to power and authority in the implementation of selected courses of action?

8. What are the most common constraints found in complex decision problems? How do they affect the process of selecting a course of action to resolve the problems?

9. Is any decision problem really new? What can be learned from the history of similar situations?

10. Do policies, rules, and guidelines tend to restrain initiative in decision making? How would it be possible to formulate a policy that did not depend on past experience for its base?

11. How do you think the appropriate groups and organizations for implementing a course of action can be created? Do you think the pattern of already-existing organizations tends to make implementations less effective?

12. Is it helpful to regard the influences of unidentified parties in a decision situation (or a related decision situation) as quasi-natural? If not, how could these influences be taken into account in a more satisfactory fashion?

### REFERENCES

1. Friend, J. K., J. M. Power, and C. J. L. Yewlett. *Public Planning: The Inter-Corporate Dimension.* London: Tavistock Publications, 1974, pp. 22–57.

2. Emery, F. E., and E. L. Trist. "The Causal Texture of Organizational Environments." *Human Relations* 18 (1965): 21–32. Reprinted in *Systems Thinking,* edited by F. E. Emery. Baltimore, Md.: Penguin Books, 1969, pp. 241–57.

3. Kroll, Morton. "Policy and Administration." In *Policies, Decisions and Organizations,* edited by F. J. Lyden, G. A. Shipman, and M. Kroll. New York: Appleton-Century-Crofts, 1969, pp. 8–27.

4. Lowi, Theodore. "Decision Making Versus Policy Making: Toward an Antidote for Technocracy." *Public Administration Review* 30 (1970): 314–25.

5. Friend, J. K., J. M. Power, and C. J. L. Yewlett. *Public Planning,* op. cit., pp. 56–57.

6. Ibid., p. 27.
7. Simon, Herbert A. *Administrative Behavior*. New York: The Free Press (paperback edition), 1965, p. 88.
8. Williams, John. *Augustus*. New York: The Viking Press, 1972, pp. 75–76.
9. Braybrooke, D. *Traffic Congestion Goes Through the Issue Machine*. London: Routledge & Kegan Paul, Ltd., 1974.
10. Tannenbaum, Robert. "Managerial Decision Making." *The Journal of Business* 23–24 (1959–1961): 31–32.
11. Archibald, K. A. "Three Views of the Experts' Role in Policy Making: Systems Analysis, Incrementalism, and the Clinical Approach." *Policy Sciences* 1 (1970): 73–86.
12. Stoessinger, John G. *Why Nations Go To War*. New York: St. Martins Press, 1974, pp. 27–30 and 223–30.

# 3

# First Steps in Dealing with a Complex Decision Problem

**INTRODUCTION**

The first steps that can be taken to deal with a complex problem are concerned with: (a) gathering information upon which an appreciation of the existing situation can be based; (b) formulating courses of action designed to transform the existing situation into one that is judged more desirable; and (c) establishing preferences between alternative courses of action. Although these steps have been listed sequentially, they are essentially inseparable in actual practice. In the case of the most complex decision problems, the processes of understanding the problem and of establishing a range of feasible courses of action for which the participant involved has a set of preferences are inextricably intertwined.

It is interesting to note that the three steps listed above comprise most of the work involved in reaching a decision in dealing with less complex problems. They would, in fact, be sufficient to resolve more complex problems were it not for the presence of more than one participant or the need to satisfy more than one objective. These latter factors require that account be taken of the interaction between sets of preferences of different participants (or with respect to different objectives). The second and third phases of the treatment of complex decision problems, discussed in Chapters 4 and 5, are concerned with that interaction.

In order to facilitate detailed consideration of the first and other phases of the treatment of complex problems, it is convenient to make two temporary simplifications at this stage. First, the steps taken in dealing with a complex problem will be discussed from the point of view of one participant in the problem, rather than from the overall point of view adopted to this point in the text. This is not to say that the existence of the other participants and their different views of the problem will be forgotten. It is merely simpler to view the situation from the standpoint of one participant at this stage and to introduce the complications caused by the involvement of other participants at a later time.

Second, the changing and dynamic character of complex problems will be ignored for the time being, in order that the basic processes involved can be discerned and examined in detail. This is the equivalent of dividing time into slices and examining one slice at this time. It is analogous to stopping a movie film at one frame for detailed consideration of its contents and restarting the action at a later time. Once again, the dynamic nature of complex decision problems will not be forgotten. It will be given full consideration in the discussion of a model of the treatment of such problems in Chapter 6.

## INFORMATION GATHERING

The feature of complex decision problems that is all-pervasive is that the information available to participants concerning a problem is incomplete. This is the feature that presents the most difficulty to those engaged in the resolution of such problems. It is natural, therefore, that the first step that participants take towards resolution is to review existing knowledge of the problem and to gather as much additional information as available time and resources allow. Information that is likely to be of the greatest value in the process of resolution is that referring to the components of the decision problem discussed in the preceding chapter. In particular, it concerns: (a) the participants, their value systems, intentions, power to influence the outcome, and relationships, and (b) the elements of the environment and the manner in which they are changing.

Information that can be collected by a participant falls into two broad categories:

1. quantitative data resulting from measurements and observation of factors pertinent to the decision situation. These data relate

mainly to the technological aspects of the environment and to the history of past trends, natural events, and quasi-natural phenomena. The purpose of collecting such data is to obtain a base from which forecasts of future conditions that relate to the factors measured or observed can be made;

2. information of a more qualitative nature regarding the less-easily-measurable elements of the environment, such as the characteristics of the participants and the social elements of the environment. This information most often takes the form of opinions, estimates, and inferences derived from observations by those involved in (or closely connected with) the decision problem.

The usefulness of information in these two categories in the treatment of complex decision problems will now be considered in more detail.

## PREDICTIONS FROM QUANTITATIVE DATA

The main use for quantitative data resulting from a program of observations or measurements is in predicting future conditions from a study of the past behavior of a number of contributing factors. The methods of prediction that can be used are reported in technical literature under the general heading of technological forecasting. These methods can be used to predict developments in the spheres of economic, sociological, and demographic change, as well as to forecast technological changes in a wide range of applied sciences. There have been a number of comprehensive descriptions of the methods of technological forecasting in the literature and the reader is referred to these for a detailed description of the methodology.[1, 2]

The methods of technological forecasting fall into three broad categories, the nature of which can be summarized as follows:

· *Use of Growth Curves*, in which a mathematical function is fitted to the historical data from which an extrapolation is made with regard to future values of the parameters concerned. Simple curve fitting techniques are used and if sufficient data are available, statistically significant estimates of the parameters involved can be made. The method is subjective in part, since the forecaster must make a choice of the type of the curve to be fitted. Furthermore, there is no guarantee that future conditions will be an extension of the past, particularly in cases where growth tends to approach a limit or discontinuity of some kind;

· *Trend Analysis,* which is applicable particularly to technological advances. Since these advances are most often logical and step-by-step, new technology usually provides developments that transcend the limitations of previous approaches. Trend analysis endeavors to forecast the level of performance that will be reached by the new technical advance. This is done by studying the history of progression of successive technical advances in a given area and determining a rate of innovation. The forecast is made by assuming that this rate of innovation will continue in the future;

· *Analytical Models,* in which the parameters that have a significant effect on future developments are specified, together with the cause-effect relationships between them. A model of this type must include both parameters that are internal to the system being studied and that can be deduced from a past state (the "endogenous" variables) and those that are external to it and cannot be deduced from a past state of the system (the "exogenous" variables). Models of this nature that truly represent very complex technical situations are difficult to construct. However, some success has been achieved in simpler situations in which enough past experience has been built up to provide a clear view of the factors involved and the relationships between them.

The methods of technological forecasting are useful in the treatment of complex decision problems in that they provide means of estimating (a) future values of factors that may act as constraints limiting the courses of action available to one or more of the participants, and (b) the probability of occurrence of a natural event or phenomenon that may form part of the future environment of the decision problem. The methods do not, of course, allow the prediction of an outcome with certainty. Their use is no sure protection against surprise with regard to future conditions and events. However, if they are used prudently, they can provide the decision maker with information on which he can base his subjective judgements of the future and with a basis for estimates of the likely probability of occurrence of future events and conditions.

### Cross Impact Analysis

The phenomenon studied in a technological forecast is often influenced by more than one major factor. These factors may not be independent, as is often assumed for simplicity in forecasting. They may have a common cause or be interrelated in some other way. To neglect these interdependencies is to risk making a serious error in forecasting. However, it is usually beyond the scope of available effort to list all potential interactions between factors that influence a situation and the nature of these interactions. Normally all that can be achieved is an estimate of the *cross impacts* between events and developments. This can be expressed in terms of the increase or decrease in the probability of a subsequent event occurring produced by the occurrence or nonoccurrence of a predecessor event.[3, 4]

Consider, for example, four events $E_1$, $E_2$, $E_3$, and $E_4$ that have estimated probabilities of occurring $p_1$, $p_2$, $p_3$, and $p_4$. There are three broad categories into which the effect of the occurrence of one of these events may affect any of the others. It may (a) enhance the probability of another event, (b) inhibit another event, or it may (c) be unrelated and therefore have no interactive effect. This can be illustrated in a matrix as shown in Table 3.1.

Table 3.1 ELEMENTARY CROSS IMPACT MATRIX

| If this event were to occur | the probability of this event would be | | | |
|---|---|---|---|---|
| | $E_1$ | $E_2$ | $E_3$ | $E_4$ |
| $E_1$ | | unchanged | enhanced | inhibited |
| $E_2$ | inhibited | | enhanced | inhibited |
| $E_3$ | enhanced | enhanced | | unchanged |
| $E_4$ | enhanced | inhibited | inhibited | |

An alternative form of cross impact matrix is shown in Table 3.2. In preparing this matrix, the events $E_1$, $E_2$, $E_3$, and $E_4$ are assumed to be in chronological order; that is $E_1$ is earlier than $E_2$, $E_2$ than $E_3$, and so on. This is indicated by showing the periods $T_1$, $T_2$, $T_3$, and $T_4$, in which the events are assumed to have the probabilities $p_1$, $p_2$, $p_3$, and $p_4$ of occurring. The diagonal cells are meaningless and are hatched in as before. However, in the cells *above* the diagonal, the interaction that takes place if the row (earlier) event occurs is shown. In the cells *below* the diagonal the interaction that takes place if the column (earlier) event *does not* take place is indicated. Estimates of the strength of the interaction and the time lag between the earlier event and its impact on the later event are shown. The description of the mode of interaction is also expanded from "enhanced, inhibited, unchanged" to "enhanced, inhibited, unchanged, prevented, and necessitated."

Table 3.2    MODIFIED CROSS IMPACT MATRIX

*EVENT OCCURS*

| Event | Period | Probability | $E_1$ | $E_2$ | $E_3$ | $E_4$ |
|-------|--------|-------------|-------|-------|-------|-------|
| $E_1$ | $T_1$ | $p_1$ | | enhanced +40% 1 year | inhibited −30% 4 years | unchanged |
| $E_2$ | $T_2$ | $p_2$ | inhibited −20% 2 years | | prevented immediate | unchanged |
| $E_3$ | $T_3$ | $p_3$ | enhanced +10% immediate | enhanced +20% 2 years | | necessitated 3 years |
| $E_4$ | $T_4$ | $p_4$ | unchanged | unchanged | prevented 2 years | |

*EVENT DOES NOT OCCUR*

This matrix can be read in the following manner. If $E_1$ actually occurs, it enhances the probability of $E_2$, the impact is to make $E_2$ 40 percent more likely, but the impact will not be felt until one year after $E_1$ occurs. On the other hand, if $E_1$ does not occur, the probability of $E_2$ occurring is inhibited, the impact is to make $E_2$ 20 percent less likely, and the effect will be felt in two years. Similar relationships between earlier and later events can be read off in the same manner.

Cross impact analysis of this sort omits many important factors. For example, interactions of higher order than one event on another are neglected, as well as interactions of combinations of events on other events or combinations. In decision situations where many events must be considered, it is practically impossible to take the very large number of such interactions into account. Together with the pitfalls of estimating probabilities and likely times of occurrence of single events, this imposes serious limitations on the reliance that can be placed on the analysis. However, it is often used as a checklist or as a basis for structuring discussion of the probability of occurrence of natural and quasi-natural events in complex decision problems and, in this respect, it is a useful technique.

## GATHERING QUALITATIVE INFORMATION

In addition to gathering quantitative data on the technical factors involved, participants in complex decision problems may wish to seek the opinions and assessments of others not directly involved in the problem as a means of confirming or modifying their own views. The information sought in such circumstances is usually broad and qualitative in nature. It may be gathered by means of informal conversations, by the use of questionnaires, or by forming a group or committee that is charged with providing the decision maker with information, experience, and advice concerning the problem. Whatever the means of gathering the information and whatever the relationship between those providing it, the objective is to pool the information available and to provide a wider range of information, experience, and judgement as a basis for the work of resolution of the problem.

A participant who is seeking the opinions of colleagues and staff members has a choice to make concerning the method of data gathering that he will adopt. He may regard reliance on informal contacts as too haphazard. On the other hand, he may be concerned about a number of difficulties that can arise in groups and committees in which the members meet fact-to-face, namely:[5]

- the greater the number of members, the greater the possible amount of misinformation, although hopefully much of this can be cancelled out by pertinent information brought forward by others;
- pressures experienced by members of a group in face-to-face meetings may affect the collection of information; for example, the views of a more vocal or a more senior member may be given more weight than his experience and judgement merit;
- views and opinions that are markedly different from those of the majority of the group may come to be discounted in group discussions;
- members of the group or a substantial portion of the group may have vested interests in certain points of view: in particular, members who have initially presented certain lines of information and thought may not be willing to relinquish them at a later time for fear of losing status in the group;
- the members of the group may have been selected unwittingly from a common subculture or school of thought, so that what ap-

pears to be a group view, in fact, represents only one of a number of possible positions.

A method designed to retain the advantages of multi-person information gathering while avoiding these disadvantages was originally put forward by Gordon and Helmer and called Delphi.[6] It has since been discussed in many articles and books.[7, 8, 9, 10] With these detailed treatments available, only a basic outline of the method necessary to the present discussion will be given here.

### The Delphi Method

The Delphi method is a means for the systematic gathering and assembly of information held by a number of individuals on a given subject. The procedure consists of submitting a sequence of questionnaires to the individuals concerned in a number of rounds. The first questionnaire is usually introductory and unspecific in nature. For example, in dealing with a complex decision situation it might pose questions about the components of the problem such as the participants, the relationships between them, and possible natural events in a given time period. It is important that the questions posed in the first round not be too structured or restrictive, in order that important factors that are outside the knowledge of the director of the inquiry may come to light.

The replies to the first questionnaire are returned to the director (usually, but not necessarily, anonymously) and he consolidates them into a single set. The consolidated information is then used as the basis of the questionnaire in round two, which seeks to gather more details on those items that are judged to be important to the problem at hand. For example, questions might be included that are designed to obtain opinions on the likely plans, objectives, and available courses of action of participants mentioned in the first-round replies. Estimates of the effects of natural and quasi-natural events might be sought as well as a forecast estimating the probabilities of such occurrences in a given time period. It is important to note that, in addition to posing questions, the second and succeeding questionnaires provide respondents with information about the views and opinions of the others involved even though they do not meet face to face. The questions in these later questionnaires are designed to amplify and investigate the opinions deduced from the first questionnaire, as well as to verify the validity of the summary of opinions derived from the replies in the previous round. The procedure continues over a number of rounds (usually between three and five) with increasingly specific questions until sufficiently detailed information has been gathered. It is not necessary to limit the inquiry to only one group of similarly qualified or positioned individuals. Questionnaires can be sent to a number of groups with different fields of knowledge or at different levels in an organization or community and the responses combined or kept separate after each round.

Delphi has two characteristics that distinguish it from other methods of information gathering, namely (a) *anonymity,* by which the individuals providing the information do not need to be known to one another and do not meet in a group discussion; this provides the opportunity for those taking part to change their opinions without loss of face; and (b) *iteration with feedback,* referring to the manner in which information is gathered in a sequence of rounds and the results of previous rounds are fed back to the individuals involved at the start of each new round of questioning. Delphi is, therefore, a means of establishing a group communication structure without encountering some of the disadvantages of data gathering in a face-to-face meeting of qualified individuals that were listed earlier. It also has clear advantages over other methods of data gathering from groups when (a) opinions are needed from a larger number of individuals than can be accommodated in a face-to-face meeting; (b) differences of opinion are so great that face-to-face encounters result in unproductive arguments; (c) the individuals involved are separated by large distances; or (d) face-to-face meetings would involve too large an expenditure of time.

Delphi can be used also to complement the discussions of a group dealing with a complex decision problem. The system provides members of the group with an opportunity to enter opinions and views anonymously, thus avoiding possible embarrassment and disapproval by the group when a contrary or widely different position is taken. Delphi also extends the gathering of views and opinions to individuals and groups not normally charged with resolution of the particular problem.

As a simple example of the use of the Delphi technique, suppose that it has been decided that a new facility such as a factory, power station, freeway, or airport is needed and several possible sizes of facility are being considered. Each alternative has certain characteristics that can be investigated such as cost, efficiency in providing the product or service desired, disruption experienced by local residents, interference with the ecology, production of pollutants, destruction of natural scenic beauty, and so on. It is required that the best sized facility be chosen taking all points of view into account. Note that in this simplified problem, the question of whether or not the facility is actually required is not included, although this might well be part of a larger interconnected problem.

The first-round Delphi questionnaire in this problem (named the Construction of Facility X) might be as shown in Figure 3.1. Successful administration of the inquiry requires attention to a number of matters. These range from an accurate spelling of the names and addresses of the respondents to the inclusion of a return address and a date by which a reply is expected. These will not be discussed in detail here.

Once the replies to the first round questionnaire have been received and collated, the second questionnaire can be prepared, as shown in Figure 3.2. Note that information from these replies is included in the second questionnaire as an introduction to questions that are designed to expand the degree of detail requested. Furthermore, the area of questioning is directed to the constituents of the decision problem once the more general subject of the nature of the problem has been addressed.

The third-round questionnaire (shown in Figure 3.3) provides information from second-round replies regarding the participants and natural events and again extends the area of inquiry by asking more detailed questions. This process is continued in as many later rounds as is thought necessary to obtain the information required without the respondents losing interest.

One result of this data gathering by Delphi might be the identification of participants and the enumeration of some very broad courses of action considered feasible by the group as shown in Table 3.3. Information on possible natural events that would affect the decision process can also be included in such a table.

### SELECTING COURSES OF ACTION FOR DETAILED CONSIDERATION

A program of information gathering such as that just described is likely to result in the proposal of a large number of possible courses of action. Many of these may come to be discarded after a preliminary examination on grounds of infeasibility with respect to the problem under consideration. However, many feasible courses of action may remain and some method is required of determining whether each of these is desirable and appropriate to the problem. Note that each participant must not only assess the courses of action open to him, but must also make similar judgements regarding the

## QUESTIONNAIRE NO. 1

Please describe on one sheet of paper your perception of the main characteristics of the decision problem known as "Construction of Facility X," giving details of any aspects that you think may present unusual difficulties.

*Answer*

Please return this to the enquiry director by . . . . . . . . . . . . . . . . .
It is not necessary to sign this sheet or identify yourself unless you feel that it is desirable that you do so.

**Figure 3.1** *First-Round Delphi Questionnaire*

1. The following problem description has been written **after** studying the responses to the first questionnaire:

    It is necessary to install a major facility in this area that will cause disruption to existing communities, may have an unpleasing exterior, and may produce dangerous and polluting effluents. Resistance to the installation is to be expected from a number of directions. The problem is to choose a size and design for the facility that will meet needs and also cause minimal protest from those affected.

    Do you agree that this is the problem? Are there any **aspects** that you would add, expand, deemphasize, or delete?

2. Who do you think are the parties with major potential to influence the resolution of this problem?

3. What major events that could influence the resolution of **this** problem do you think might occur in the next few years?

Figure 3.2  *Second-Round Delphi Questionnaire*

1. The parties suggested in the responses to the second questionnaire as having major potential to influence the problem under consideration are:

> *The Project Group*, which has proposed the installation and which will be charged with carrying it out
>
> *Citizens Protest Groups*, consisting of local residents who may be affected by the installation and others such as ecologists and conservationists
>
> *Elected Representatives*, whose support and active intervention may be sought by the citizens protest groups
>
> *Government*, which must authorize the installation at a number of different levels and possibly provide all or part of the funding.

Please review this list and suggest

   (a) any other major participants
   (b) any subgroups within your list of major participants
   (c) any courses of action you think might be available to each of these participants in the immediate future.

2. The possible natural events suggested in the second questionnaire were:

> *Recession* in the economy resulting in decreased demand for the product or service*
>
> *Disaster* at a similar facility elsewhere casting doubt on the safety of the proposed facility
>
> *Technological Development* resulting in the facility becoming relatively less efficient or obsolescent.

Please review this list and provide:

   (a) any other natural events that you think might occur during the period of implementation and the lifetime of the facility
   (b) your estimate of the probability of occurrence of these events in the next   (i) 1 year   (ii) 3 years   (iii) 5 years.

* product of a factory or power plant, service from a freeway or airport

Figure 3.3   *Third-Round Delphi Questionnaire*

Table 3.3   A First Listing of Participants and Courses of Action

| Participants | Available Courses of Action |
| --- | --- |
| Project Group | Continue construction of large facility<br>Build small facility<br>Settle for mid-size facility |
| Citizens' Protest | Support government in election<br>Picket construction site<br>Settle for mid-size facility |
| Elected Representatives | Support Citizens' Protest |
| Government | Provide support to Project Group |
| Possible Natural Events | Recession<br>Disaster<br>Technological Development |

courses of action that the other participants would think to be appropriate.

There have been a number of methods suggested to provide guidance to individuals in the process of selecting courses of action in different types of decision problems. One such method is presented in the strategy of *incrementalism*.[11, 12] The main theme of incrementalism is that there is a large class of decision problems in which the decision maker should concentrate his search for appropriate courses of action on those that will achieve situations that are marginally different from the existing situation. The type of decision problems to which the incremental approach is appropriate include those arising in situations in which (a) the results of past policies and courses of action have been satisfactory and (b) the nature of the problem and the means for dealing with it have not changed significantly from previous occurrences of a similar nature. Adherents to the incrementalist strategy justify its use in these circumstances on the following grounds:

- the more a possible future state represents a departure from the present situation, the more difficult it is to predict the consequences of actions designed to achieve that state. For this reason radical actions may be less acceptable than those designed to achieve more modest objectives;

- the strategy allows considerable simplification of the decision making process by omitting consideration of nonincremental

.courses of action and by requiring evaluation only of those consequences of a course of action that can be readily deduced from
comparison with the status quo;

since only marginal extensions of the status quo are considered,
comparison of two courses of action involves matters that are
relatively familiar and well understood; even when matters are
not well understood, incrementalism leaves enough institutional
insurance in force to allow retrieval of mistakes.

Critics of incrementalism say that the strategy is not appropriate
when (a) the objectives, values, constraints, and other elements of
the decision problem are changing rapidly, and (b) when a radically
new means of resolution of a problem (such as a major technological
development) has become available for the first time. Many are concerned about the impact of incrementalism on such activities as
policy making, fearing that if it were widely adopted, it might rein-
force the elements of inertia and anti-innovation that appear in all
human endeavors.[13, 14, 15]

The proponents of incrementalism do not claim universal applicability for their strategy.[16] They specifically exclude extraordinary
decision situations such as "revolutionary decision making" and
"grand opportunities" from the spectrum of conditions under which
incrementalism is expected to be appropriate. These are decision
situations that have been termed "fundamental" by Etzioni.[17] Fundamental decisions are those that are not concerned with marginal
movements from the status quo. They are decisions that change the
course of the affairs of those concerned in some decisive way. The
decisions to close a manufacturing plant, to market a completely new
product, or to introduce a radically new policy are examples of such
fundamental decisions. They are usually characterized by the relatively high cost associated with reversing the selected course of action
once a start has been made on implementation.

Etzioni contends that fundamental decisions and those that should
be approached by the incrementalist strategy are usually closely
linked. Fundamental decisions are often preceded by a series of incremental ones that lead up to the larger and more wide-ranging
step. If this occurs, the fundamental decision may not seem as radical
as it might have if it were announced without the warning afforded
by the incremental steps. This phenomenon has often been used by
those in authority to soften the blow of an unpopular fundamental
decision. On the other hand, fundamental decisions often provide the
context and impetus for a series of later incremental decisions that
serve to implement the original larger step. These later incremental
decisions exist solely by virtue of the change of state brought about

by the earlier fundamental decision. While the total number of fundamental decisions may be very much smaller, their impact is significantly greater. Fundamental decisions provide a mechanism of preventing the aimless drift that many critics of incrementalism regard as the major disadvantage of that strategy.

Etzioni proposed a method of proceeding in the face of a complex decision problem (called *mixed-scanning*) that recognizes the existence of both fundamental and incremental types of decision. In applying the mixed scanning strategy, a broad survey of the problem is undertaken first in which it is hoped that any fundamental decisions will be revealed and broad courses of action appropriate to them designated. In a second stage of the mixed scanning process incremental courses of action are identified. By use of two or more levels of scanning, courses of action appropriate to all aspects of the problem and all time periods can be identified.

The relative investment of time and effort between the various levels of the mixed scanning process depends on the nature of the problem situation, on the judgement of the decision maker involved, on the cost of additional detailed scanning, and on the relative cost attached to missing a necessary fundamental or incremental decision. The strategy is not limited to only two levels of scanning. Three or more levels can be used if this is considered necessary in the light of the experience of the decision maker. Furthermore, the number of levels of scanning employed need not be constant, nor need any one particular level be employed continuously. In practice, the mixed scanning procedure may encompass work at a number of levels in rotation so that no level of consideration is neglected for any period of time while, at the same time, no level is given exclusive attention to the detriment of the others.

## GENERATION OF SCENARIOS

Combinations of courses of action available to the participants define several possible situations or scenarios. For example, if "yes" is written against each course of action shown in Table 3.3 if it is actually selected for implementation and "no" if it is not, the scenario resulting from any combination of selections by the participants can be described by reading down the column of "yes's" and "no's." As an illustration, the scenario marked "Current" in Table 3.4 is that in which the Project Group continues preparation for construction of a large facility, does not build a small facility and does not settle for a mid-size facility. The Citizens' Protest Group seeks to delay the project by picketing the construction site while, for the time being, supporting the government, and not settling for a mid-size facility. The Elected Representatives support the citizens while the Government provides support to the Project Group.

A future scenario that might be the basis of a settlement of the decision problem is shown in the column marked "Possible Settlement." Reading downwards, it can be described as a scenario in which the Project Group settles for a mid-size facility while discontinuing actions that would lead to a large or a small facility, the Citizens' Protest lifts its pickets from the construction site while agreeing to the mid-sized facility and continuing to support the Government in the forthcoming election. The Elected Representatives continue to support the Citizens while the Government continues to support the Project Group in its decision to opt for a mid-size facility.

The possible occurrence of natural and quasi-natural events and phenomena can be shown in the Table and included in scenarios in

Table 3.4    GENERATION OF SCENARIOS IN THE
CONSTRUCTION OF FACILITY X

| Participants | Available Courses of Action | Examples of Scenarios | |
| --- | --- | --- | --- |
| | | Current | Possible Settlement |
| Project Group | Continue construction of large facility | yes | no |
| | Build small facility | no | no |
| | Settle for mid-size facility | no | yes |
| Citizens' Protest | Support government in election | yes | yes |
| | Picket construction site | yes | no |
| | Settle for mid-size facility | no | yes |
| Elected Representatives | Support citizens' protest | yes | yes |
| Government | Provide support to Project Group | yes | yes |
| Possible Natural Events | Recession | no | no |
| | Disaster | no | ? |
| | Technological development | no | no |

the same way as are the available courses of action. In Table 3.4, for example, three possible natural or quasi-natural events are included, described by the titles "Recession," "Disaster," and "Technological Development." The "no's" against these possible events in the "Current" column denote that none of them is part of the current scenario. In the "Possible Settlement" scenario, the column indicates that the settlement proposed is applicable to conditions in which no recession or technological development has taken place, but that the effect of a disaster is open to question at the present time.

In practical analysis, it is more convenient in preparing tables such as Table 3.4, to write a *1* for a course of action that is implemented and a *0* against one that is not implemented in the particular scenario being described. A scenario is then represented by a column of *1*'s and *0*'s as in Table 3.5, which is derived from Table 3.4 by replacing the word "yes" by a *1* and the word "no" by a *0*. The number of combinations of even the small number of available courses of action shown in Table 3.5 is very large. In fact the number of such combinations of the eight courses of action shown is 256. Not all the future scenarios represented by these combinations are necessarily likely to come about or important to consider. Some may not even be feasible. For example, it is presumably not feasible for the Project Group to build a small facility and to settle for a mid-sized facility at the same time. Examples of infeasibilities of this sort are shown at the right hand side of Table 3.5.

It is important to note that, in actual practice, scenarios generated by a participant are based on his own perception of the problem and additionally on his perception of the other participants' available courses of action. Others involved in the problem may view the range of future situations differently, depending on their available information and on the nature of their perceptions, intentions, and attitudes. Differences in the perceptions of participants of possible future scenarios play an important part in the process of resolution of complex decision problems. These differences are the major reason why communication between participants is an essential part of that process.

## ESTABLISHING PREFERENCES BETWEEN
## FUTURE SCENARIOS

Having gathered as much information as possible and formulated a number of future scenarios based on that information, participants in a complex decision situation are eventually faced with the task of

Table 3.5 THE CONSTRUCTION OF FACILITY X
PARTICIPANTS, AVAILABLE COURSES OF ACTION AND SCENARIOS

| Participants | Available Courses of Action | Examples of Scenarios | | Examples of Infeasibles |
|---|---|---|---|---|
| | | Current | Possible Settlement | |
| Project Group | Continue construction of large facility | 1 | 0 | 1 1 |
| | Build small facility | 0 | 0 | 1 1 1 |
| | Settle for mid-size facility | 0 | 1 | 1 1 |
| Citizens' Protest | Support government in election | 1 | 1 | |
| | Picket construction site | 1 | 0 | 1 |
| | Settle for mid-size facility | 0 | 1 | 1 |
| Elected Representatives | Support citizens' protest | 1 | 1 | |
| Government | Provide support to Project Group | 1 | 1 | |
| Possible Natural Events | Recession | 0 | 0 | |
| | Disaster | 0 | ? | |
| | Technological development | 0 | 0 | |

54

determining their preferences between the alternative future situations that they perceive as being available to them.

There is little explicit guidance available from literature to assist those faced with this task. Simon, for example, recommends that the decision maker examine future scenarios until he discovers one that he judges to be "good enough" according to a criterion based on his values and expectations.[18] In his exposition of mixed scanning, Etzioni recommends a review of available alternatives and elimination of those against which there are "crippling objections."[19] However, he offers no prescription to the decision maker to guide him in the task of deciding the basis on which objections are to be evaluated. The advice given to incrementalists is hardly more explicit. The recommendation to those adopting that strategy is that marginal movements be made away from any situation that is regarded as undesirable.[20] However, as Etzioni points out, the judgement of what is undesirable and which direction constitutes a move towards a more desirable situation is necessarily particular to the participant and dependent on such of his characteristics as his value system and his perception of the problem.[21]

Preferences between future scenarios are, therefore, usually established by each participant on the basis of his own judgement and experience. There are, however, a number of analytical techniques for establishing preferences in the presence of multiple objectives that may be of some practical assistance to those faced with this task.[22] The actual applicability of any one of these techniques depends upon the amount of quantitative information available in the particular problem under consideration. In particular, the applicability of these techniques depends on whether or not the information is available in a well-defined and acceptable form in the following areas:

1. quantitative measures relating to the degree of achievement of each of the objectives;

2. a relationship between the units in which these measures are expressed that allows aggregation of achievement towards the various objectives into an overall performance measure;

3. numerical weighting factors describing the relative priorities and preferences between the objectives.

The techniques fall into three broad classes, each of which is applicable only when certain of the above information is available. These classes and the information necessary for their use are shown in Table 3.6.

Table 3.6    Techniques for Establishing Preferences and
Attendant Necessary Conditions

| Class of Technique | Necessary Available Information Before Technique Can Be Used |
|---|---|
| Weighting Methods | 1. Well-understood quantitative measures related to each objective<br>2. A direct relationship between the units in which these measures are expressed<br>3. Numerical weighting factors describing priorities between objectives |
| Minimizing Deviation from Goals | 1. Quantitative measures related to each objective, but not necessarily a relationship between units in which these measures are expressed<br>2. Numerical weighting factors describing priorities between objectives |
| Sequential Elimination | 1. Quantitative measures related to each objective, but no relationship between units or numerical weighting factors describing priorities are necessary |

The various classes of technique will now be described in more detail.

### Weighting Methods

When quantitative information in all three of the above areas is available, a multiple objective choice can be reduced in effect to a single objective choice by the combination of the numerically weighted measures relating to each objective into a single expression. This is the basis of what are usually classified as weighting methods.[23]

As a simple example of the use of the weighting method, suppose that the objectives of a project to locate a new factory or highway can be assessed in terms of minimizing cost, minimizing the number of homes to be expropriated, minimizing the extent of intrusion onto farm and recreational land, and maximizing benefits to the company or users involved. Suppose also that performance in achieving these objectives can be measured on scales that can be directly related (or more simply still, all in terms of the same quantitative parameter such as dollars) and that they can be expressed as $u_1$, $u_2$, $u_3$, and $u_4$ respectively. Further, suppose that the relative preferences between these attributes can be expressed in terms of numerical weightings $k_1$, $k_2$, $k_3$, and $k_4$. This implies, for example, that the number of homes to be expropriated and the extent of intrusion on farm and recreational land are viewed in a priority relationship defined by the ratio $k_2/k_3$. The method then provides for selection of an alternative in terms of the expression:

$$z = k_1u_1 + k_2u_2 + k_3u_3 + k_4u_4$$

This method is attractive because of its simplicity and the ease with which a basis for choice between alternatives can be obtained. However, there may not be many practical situations in which it can be applied. For example, it may be difficult to express the results of implementing a particular course of action in terms of a well-defined measure of effectiveness or benefit. Many problems arising in government are of this type. For example, it is difficult to express the benefits to be obtained from a program to increase public library holdings or a course of action to improve the welfare of the disadvantaged in this form. Many decisions at the senior levels of private corporations encounter this same difficulty. For example, those decisions concerned with improvements in employee working conditions or in relations with the local community are not usually expressible in purely quantitative form.

Further difficulties may arise in expressing the benefits of a course of action with respect to each of a number of objectives in the same units of measurement. For example, there may be no common unit in which the benefits of eliminating grade crossings and providing unemployment insurance can be measured. Setting quantitative weighting factors between the achievement of different objectives often poses similar difficulties. For example, it may be very difficult (if not impossible) to agree on a quantitative measure of the relative priority of assistance to the poor and national defense. Such difficulties arise even in organizations where profit is the prime objective. It may not be possible, for example, to set quantitative priorities between such objectives as the attainment of profits in the current period and diversification over the longer term.

### Minimization of Deviation from Goals

Methods exist that are applicable when information is available in only two of the three areas listed earlier. Suppose that it is possible to find quantitative measures relating to the degree of achievement of each of the objectives and to specify numerical weightings expressing priorities between objectives. Suppose, however, that not all the measures of achievement are expressible in the same units. For example, in the situation discussed earlier in this chapter, the intrusion into farmland may be measured in acres and the number of homes expropriated in housing units. It may be impossible or unacceptable to express these measures in a common unit such as dollars.

A method that can be used in these circumstances is based on consideration of the deviations of the measured contribution of each alternative from goals that are set for each objective. For example in the case just discussed, the *goals* might be expressed as $\bar{u}_1$, $\bar{u}_2$, $\bar{u}_3$, and $\bar{u}_4$ and the deviations between these goals and the actual value for a given alternative as $(\bar{u}_1 - u_1)$, $(\bar{u}_2 - u_2)$, $(\bar{u}_3 - u_3)$, and $(\bar{u}_4 - u_4)$. With the weighting factors between attributes $k_1$, $k_2$, $k_3$, and $k_4$ as before, the choice between alternatives is made in terms of the expression

$$k_1(\bar{u}_1 - u_1) + k_2(\bar{u}_2 - u_2) + k_3(\bar{u}_3 - u_3) + k_4(\bar{u}_4 - u_4).$$

Note that it is the weighted deviation from goals that is being minimized here, rather than the sum of achieved values related to objectives. The multiple objective problem has therefore been reduced to a single objective problem by substituting the single objective of minimizing the weighted sum of deviations from goals for the multiple objectives of optimizing the value of each of the attributes. A more complex technique based on the same principle in which a continuous range of alternatives can be compared in this fashion is known as "goal programming."[24]

### Sequential Elimination Methods

In many cases when preferences must be established between alternatives, quantitative information is not available in two of the areas listed earlier. These are cases in which acceptable measures of benefits can be established relative to each of the objectives, but in which neither common units for these measures nor numerical weighting factors between objectives can be specified. In such circumstances one of the various sequential elimination methods may be of some assistance in establishing preferences between alternatives.[25]

Suppose, for example, in the case of the location of a factory or a highway discussed earlier, certain necessary levels can be specified against each of the objectives, as follows:

*Cost*    Total cost of project not to exceed $X
          Total cost of land acquisition not to exceed $Y

*Homes*    Number of residential properties destroyed not to exceed
          $N_1$
          Number of farm properties expropriated not to exceed $N_2$
*Intrusion* Acres of farmland lost not to exceed $A_1$
          Acres of recreation land lost not to exceed $A_2$
*Benefits*  Maximum benefits in any year not to be less than $B_1$
          Average benefits over 10 years not to be less than $B_2$

Sets of criteria can be constructed from these requirements by use of the conjunctive "AND," the disjunctive "OR," and combinations of them as shown, for example, in Table 3.7.

Table 3.7    CRITERIA FOR USE IN SEQUENTIAL ELIMINATION

| Cost | Homes | Intrusion | Benefits |
|------|-------|-----------|----------|
| Cost of project not to exceed $X | Number of residential properties destroyed not to exceed $N_1$ | Acres of farmland lost not to exceed $A_1$ | Maximum benefits in any year not to be less than $B_1$ |
| AND | AND | OR | OR |
| Cost of land acquisition not to exceed $Y | Number of farm properties expropriated not to exceed $N_2$ | Acres of recreation land lost not to exceed $A_2$ | Average benefits over 10 years not to be less than $B_2$ |
| | | | OR |
| | | | Maximum benefits not to be less than $B_1$ AND average benefits not to be less than $B_2$ |

Alternatives can now be judged in each of the above categories and rules can be formulated for elimination of those that do not meet the necessary criteria. For example, those alternatives that fail the criteria in all four categories might be eliminated first, followed by those that fail all the criteria in three categories, and so on, until only one remains. Another method of elimination involves ranking the criteria related to objectives in order of importance and the comparison of alternatives in the first instance against the criterion afforded highest importance. If a single alternative is highest in judged performance against the most important attribute, it is chosen. If a tie results between two or more alternatives, the process is repeated in terms of the second most important attribute, and so on.

### Nonquantitative Ranking of Alternatives

In many practical situations in which complex decision problems are encountered, there is insufficient reliable information available in each of the three areas listed earlier to allow use of any of the foregoing quantitative techniques of comparison. In such circumstances, those involved must rely mainly on their experience and judgement in establishing nonquantitative (ordinal) preferences between alternatives. Ordinal preferences provide a ranking of alternatives against each objective, but no quantitative expression of how much one alternative is preferred to any other.

It is possible to use a form of the sequential elimination technique when only ordinal preferences between alternatives are available, although the method has much less force in such cases. Suppose, for example, that there are five alternatives (A,B,C,D, and E) and four objectives and that the alternatives can be ranked in order of preference against each objective as shown in Table 3.8.

Table 3.8    RANKING BY PREFERENCE AGAINST OBJECTIVES

| | | Objective | | |
|---|---|---|---|---|
| | 1 | 2 | 3 | 4 |
| | A | A | B | B |
| | B | D | C | A |
| | C | C | A | C |
| | D | B | D | E |
| | E | E | E | D |

If all objectives are regarded as equally important, the choice might be narrowed to that between A, B, and C after preferences had been listed explicitly as in Table 3.8. If a ranking of importance between objectives can be stated, the choice might be narrowed further. For example, if objectives 1 and 4 were of much greater importance than 2 and 3, the choice would logically lie between alternatives A and B.

At best, however, such techniques serve only to encourage explicit statements of preferences from those involved and to provide some framework within which choice can be narrowed. The ultimate basis for choice remains the judgement of the individual or individuals involved.

If the choice between alternatives can be narrowed to two, it may be possible to establish preferences by a method involving trade-offs. In the simplest application of this technique, a sheet of paper is divided in half by a vertical line. Each half is assigned to one alternative. Advantages and disadvantages of each of the alternatives with respect to each of the objectives are listed in their respective halves of the page. Factors that are judged to balance each other are then crossed out on each side of the sheet. The alternative with most advantages (or least disadvantages) remaining can then be regarded as the most preferred. Once again, this method can only be regarded as an aid to organizing thought. It does, however, provide some assistance in establishing preferences when all other methods are found to be inapplicable.

There is a temptation when dealing with ordinal rankings to assign numbers to the rankings and to establish preferences in terms of a total score. For example, five points might be assigned to the first place in a ranking such as is shown in Table 3.8, four points for a second place and so on. The total score can then be calculated for each alternative against each objective and a numerical weighting between objectives can even be introduced to arrive at a set of single numbers supposedly representing the desirability of each of the alternatives. Such methods are attractive in that they provide a simple, understandable comparison between alternatives that is derived in an apparently logical fashion. The danger involved is that numbers may be introduced arbitrarily, primarily from a desire to adopt a simple method of comparison. If this is the case, the results obtained have only as much validity as do the numerical estimates and arbitrary assignment of these numbers can lead to serious error.

## Some Aspects of Individual Behavior in Problem Perception, Formulation, and Choice

The behavior and activities of those engaged in the perception of complex problems, in the formulation of alternatives, and in the establishment of preferences between them are influenced to a greater or lesser extent by preconceived concepts of the various factors involved. These preconceived concepts are related primarily to previous experiences. They may give rise to what have been termed conceptual blocks.[26]

Conceptual blocks may be considered conveniently in the following categories:

- *Perceptual blocks,* which tend to limit the areas in which information is sought and gathered. Perceptual blocks may make it difficult for an individual to assess a problem from various viewpoints. Such blocks may result in stereotyping and labeling of individuals or actions, and the consequent introduction of biased information into the process of problem resolution;
- *Cultural and Environmental blocks,* resulting from exposure to a particular set of cultural patterns or from operation in a particular social and physical environment;
- *Emotional blocks,* such as may arise, for example, from an aversion to uncertainty and risk taking, related, possibly, to fear of failure or mistake;
- *Intellectual and Expressive blocks,* resulting in an inability to generate ideas and to communicate them to others.

Conceptual blocks generally cause a diminution of creativity in dealing with complex problems. A number of prescriptions for overcoming their effects have been put forward. These include (a) maintaining a questioning attitude, (b) adopting the practice of compiling lists of ideas and related points in note form and the continual reviewing and revision of these lists, and (c) the conscious switching between modes of thinking and between means of representing thoughts at intervals during the consideration of a problem.[27]

Prescriptions with similar intentions have been put forward by de Bono in his book on "lateral thinking."[28] He describes what is called "vertical thinking" as a process in which the search for alternatives is continued until a promising one is found, after which that course of action is pursued until there is reason to stop. By contrast, lateral thinking is said to have the aim of generating alternatives in a manner that is deliberately nonsequential and unconventional. It seeks to concentrate on dominant ideas and crucial factors, to view situations in different ways, and to restructure information in such a way that new alternatives appear. There is a conscious attempt to break with the familiar, to challenge existing concepts, and to seek different ways of looking at situations.

Lateral thinking is recommended as a method of consideration of available information that is complementary to the more conventional logical and sequential vertical thinking, rather than as a replacement for it. The two modes of thought can be used together, one covering areas that might otherwise be neglected by the other. Lateral thinking is often more appropriate at the early stages of consideration of problem situations when perceptions can be restructured as a preliminary to development of certain specific scenarios or courses of action. De Bono does not present explicit prescriptions, but relies rather on exhortations to avoid narrow considerations of problems. He suggests such techniques as (a) rotating areas of attention; (b) participating in sessions designed to provide cross-stimulation of group members; (c) breaking down situations into "fractions" and then restructuring the parts; (d) reversal of existing situations, ideas and trends "to see what happens;" and (e) challenging existing categorizations and labels. The desired effect is much the same as that sought by many other proposed techniques for maintaining the creativity of those involved in the treatment of complex problems.

## The Effect of Stress

Individuals involved in the resolution of complex decision problems are frequently subjected to stress and tension. There are a number of factors that may contribute to this stress. Foremost among them are (a) the pressure induced by the limited amount of time available for consideration of the problem before a course of action must be selected; (b) the perceived importance of the problem; (c) the uncertainty caused by possession of incomplete information; (d) the existence of a number of conflicting objectives or interest groups; (e) the possibility that courses of action might be necessary that would be unpopular with many of those affected; and (f) the fear that a chosen course of action might only serve to complicate the situation rather than to solve it. These and other factors may affect different participants involved in a complex problem in different ways, depending on each participant's characteristics and on their perceptions of the problem.

The main effects of stress over prolonged periods of time are "increased irritability, subclinical paranoid reactions, heightened suspiciousness, hostility, and increased defensiveness."[29] The effects of these reactions on performance depend upon the intensity of the stress experienced and the complexity of the task to be performed. A mild degree of stress often increases performance of simple, well-learned tasks although very intense stress often results in complete disintegration of performance. The more complex the task, the more likely that stress will disrupt the performance.

Different types of individuals react differently to various degrees of stress. Some individuals are habitually relaxed and most of the stress situations in which they are involved have the effect of enhancing their performance. On the other hand, an individual who is constantly under some form of mild stress may become partially or completely disorganized when additional pressure is placed on him.

Learning behavior is also affected by stress. Simple learning (for example, classic defense conditioning) may be facilitated by stress, whereas more complex learning is often disrupted under the same conditions. Under intense or persistent stress, it is usual that more recent and more complex behavior is replaced by more basic forms. This often involves regression to more simple perceptual and motivational processes, restricted spatial and temporal focus, and a tendency towards less fine discriminations. Stress has also been found to activate the more basic survival needs and to minimize those that are more superficial. It has been suggested also that stress tends to cause a reduction in the number and variety of the stimuli to which an individual will react. This results in a rigidity of behavior in which actions that were regarded as successful in past situations may be repeated, even if the present situation is quite different.[30]

Stress also sharpens individual behavior patterns so that characteristic traits become accentuated and dominant. A hesitant individual becomes more hesitant, and a decisive person more decisive. Relationships between an individual under stress and others are similarly distorted from the normal.

### Behavior in Groups

A number of experiments have been conducted to study the effect of stress on the relationships between individual members of a group. These experiments are at best only a representation of real-life conditions and it is important, therefore, to draw conclusions that appear to have a general (rather than a particular) nature. For example, it has been found that, as the stress on a group increases, there is often an increase in cooperation between the members, at least initially.[31] There is an accompanying decrease in the number of disagreements between the members, a decrease in the number of arguments and instances of aggressive behavior, and a reduction of self-oriented behavior on the part of the members. At the same time, there is an increase in behavior by members that would result in better and closer integration of the group.

There is evidence, however, that this move towards closer integration of the group may start to falter if it begins to appear that no generally favorable solution to the problem at hand is likely to be forthcoming.[32] This may indicate that the mutual reinforcement between the members is dependent on the expectation of a successful outcome. Once the possibility of failure becomes established in the minds of individuals, they may tend to withdraw from what they regard as unprofitable group actions and seek to take actions designed to safeguard their own interests in the situation.

A general conclusion from these experiments is that cooperation in a group is enhanced by a moderate amount of stress. Individuals become motivated to work together and to provide mutual reinforcement in what is regarded as a common cause. Too much stress is likely to reduce the integration of the group and diminish the efficiency of its work directed towards problem solving. At high levels of stress individuals may dissociate themselves from the work of the group and endeavor to work out their own solution to the problem. In these circumstances the efforts of these individuals are likely to be characterized by foreshortened perspectives, a narrowing of alternatives considered to those with which the individual is most familiar, and difficulty in thinking ahead and estimating future consequences of actions.[33]

Other studies of the activities of groups of individuals engaged in the perception and formulation of a problem and in the choice between alternatives reveal various behavioral anomalies. These appear to fall into one or more of the following categories: (a) seeming blindness to courses of action that can be shown in retrospect to have been clearly in the decision maker's interest; (b) excessive risk taking that could not be justified in view of the limited amount of information available; and (c) compliance to the views and demands of a dominant member of the group and suppression of information that indicates contrary to the desires of such a dominant member. Behavior of this sort has often contributed to gross miscalculations and major mistakes that are brought into sharp relief in studies undertaken after the fact.[34] These studies were of course conducted with all the advantages of hindsight. However, the incidence of such errors in decision making may be higher than is generally appreciated because those responsible for decisions with bad outcomes are understandably reluctant to give their results wide publicity. The fact that such examples are drawn more from public affairs than from business operations is probably due to the greater amount of information on those matters that is in the public domain.

Janis has pointed out that deficiencies in group decision making behavior are often due to faulty leadership of the group.[35] This may result in a situation in which individual members are subjected to subtle constraints (often unconsciously reinforced by leaders) that prevent them from bringing contrary information to bear on a decision process once the others in the group appear to be approaching a concensus. He calls the situation that arises in such circumstances by the Orwellian term "group-think," describing it as a mode of thinking that occurs "in a cohesive ingroup, when the members' striving for unanimity override their motivation to realistically appraise alternative courses of action."[36]

This striving for unanimity may be an intuitive reaction to the consequences of the theorem of Arrow,[37] which stipulates categorically that no general rule can be formulated governing the manner by which a group, the members of which hold substantially disparate views, should arrive at a decision. The difficulty posed by the Arrow theorem can be circumvented in several ways. For example, the group may adopt the views and preferences of one of the members. Alternatively, a convention of the members (or a subgroup of them that eventually dominates the group) may decide upon a standard set of preferences by mutual agreement. The consequences of the Arrow theorem are discussed further in Chapter 5.

### Prescriptions for Avoiding Group-Think

Janis has provided a number of prescriptions for avoiding group-think. These have some application in providing for a broad based gathering of information relevant to a decision problem.[38] These prescriptions can be summarized as follows:

- the leader of an inquiry or of a decision making group should give high priority in discussion to the airing of objections and doubts;
- the leader should be impartial at the outset and not advocate the specific courses of action he would like to see adopted;
- more than one group should work on a complex problem, with each group having a different leader; if only one group exists, it should break up into subgroups under different chairmen from time to time and then reform and exchange information;

- members of the group should discuss its proceedings on occasion with trusted associates and report their views and reactions to the group as a whole;
- one or more outside persons with expert knowledge should be invited to meetings of the group on a staggered basis and their views on proceedings to date solicited;
- at least one member should be assigned to act in the role of devil's advocate in each meeting;
- significant amounts of time in the group sessions should be spent examining information on other participants' actions, preferences, and available courses of action, and details of natural and quasi-natural events that have occurred or might occur in the future;
- once a consensus is reached, it should be reconsidered and confirmed or rejected at a later meeting held after time has been allowed for members to collect their doubts and reservations.

Janis has discussed each of these prescriptions in detail and the reader is urged to refer to his book for a comprehensive review of the advantages and possible undesirable side effects of these methods of approach to information gathering and group decision making.

## SUMMARY

One of the first steps normally taken by a decision maker faced with a complex problem is to gather and analyze information relevant to the elements of the problem situation. He can improve his appreciation of the situation by analysis of data gathered concerning past events and trends. This can be done by several methods that are well documented in the literature and that can be classified under the general heading of technological forecasting. The output of forecasting is usually in terms of an estimate of the probability of occurrence of future events. The interactions between events is often important and these can be studied by a technique known as cross impact analysis. While use of this technique does not guarantee accuracy, it can be used as a checklist and as a basis for structuring discussion concerning the likelihood of occurrence of possible natural and quasi-natural events.

More qualitative information may be sought from individuals and from groups of individuals meeting face-to-face in committee sessions or special task forces. There are certain difficulties in gathering information in this way. These result from misinformation commonly held by members of the group, pressures experienced within the group, the existence of vested interests among members, and unwitting selection of members from a common school of thought. The Delphi method can be used to supplement data gathering in face-to-face meetings and to overcome some of these difficulties. It uses a series of questionnaires that are filled out in sequence by individuals who can remain anonymous. Successive questionnaires contain information from previous responses so that the process is iterative with feedback. Delphi is a means of establishing a communication structure between individuals who are geographically separated and between numbers of people too large to accommodate in a meeting. Unproductive arguments resulting from differences of opinion are eliminated also.

The activities of information gathering, perceiving and formulating of the problem, and postulating courses of action are inseparable in practice. The number of courses of action available to the participants in a complex decision situation may be very large. Some method is required by which those that should be considered in detail can be selected. One strategy that offers some guidance in this respect is incrementalism. Adherents to this strategy consider only courses of action that result in future situations that differ marginally from the status quo. The incrementalist strategy allows considerable simplification of the decision making process as well as some economy in data gathering.

Incrementalism is generally considered to be a useful strategy when the nature of the problem and the means available for dealing with it do not change significantly. It has been held to be less acceptable in situations where a major change in the course of affairs appears to be required. For example, Etzioni has pointed out that some decision situations require courses of action designed to bring about fundamental changes. Fundamental decisions such as these are often preceded and followed by incremental ones. He put forward a method of *mixed scanning* that recognizes the existence of both fundamental and incremental decisions and prescribes a method of ensuring that they are both considered. It consists of a mix of broad surveys of the problem area and in-depth investigations of areas that are judged in the first survey to merit such attention.

In the absence of sufficient information to fabricate a comprehensive model, those faced with complex problems often turn to the construction of discrete scenarios. Scenarios are descriptions of situations in terms of their major constituents. They can be represented in a tabular form that is convenient for analysis. Consideration of scenarios allows concentration on possible future situations that are of particular interest to those involved in a decision problem.

The process of establishing preferences between alternative scenarios may be supported by quantitative analysis if (a) a quantitative measure of achievement of each objective is available; (b) all such measures are expressed in directly related units; and (c) numerical weighting factors expressing relative priorities between objectives are available. If some or all of these factors are not available, quantitative methods of comparison have much less force. Such techniques as are available for use in these circumstances are mainly aids to organizing thought. The ultimate basis for choice is the judgement of the individual or individuals involved.

Individual behavior in the perception of problems, in formulating courses of action, and in establishing preferences between them may be affected to some degree by conceptual blocks that bring about a diminution of creativity. There are certain prescriptions designed to reduce this undesirable effect that involve continual conscious switching between modes of thinking and between means of representing ideas and thoughts.

Individuals involved in complex problems are frequently exposed to stress and tension. A mild degree of stress may improve performance. However, intense or persistent stress may have disruptive effects on the activities of an individual. This is often observed in the behavior of individuals in a group. Mild stress may cause an increase of cooperation between members of a group, whereas an increase in the level of stress or its persistence over a prolonged period may cause a reduction in the integration of effort. Deficiencies in group decision making behavior are often due to faulty leadership. This can lead to a phenomenon in which pertinent information is ignored and realistic appraisal of the problem is sacrificed in order to maintain unanimity of opinion. Prescriptions against such occurrences include emphasis on the airing of doubts and objections and on methods of bringing a wide range of opinions before the group.

## DISCUSSION TOPICS

1. What is the difference between a comprehensive model of a decision situation and a set of scenarios describing certain aspects of it? Do you think the practice of generating scenarios is more appropriate to complex decision problems and if so, why?
2. What factors would you consider in making a choice between

conducting a Delphi enquiry or holding face-to-face meetings in a group information gathering activity?

3. Why is it important to include summaries of results of previous rounds in a Delphi questionnaire? How can the new questions be best related to those in previous questionnaires? What should be done in cases where opinions seem to be polarized into two groups?

4. Is anonymity essential in a Delphi enquiry? Under what circumstances would it be advantageous to reveal the authorship of responses?

5. Forecasting can be done by analogy, by use of growth curves, by trend analysis, or by analytical models. The subjectivity of the estimates is likely to decrease in the order of methods quoted, but the difficulty of the analysis is likely to increase. How would you choose between these methods and how would circumstances affect your choice?

6. Is cross impact analysis worthwhile and, if so, under what circumstances and for what purposes? Do higher order interactions make conclusions less valuable in all cases?

7. How can bias be eliminated in data gathering by an individual or by a group?

8. Can you give examples of the *group-think* phenomenon from your own experience? Does it always lead to a bad outcome? (Janis appears to say not always.)

9. Do you think that group-think is an intuitive reaction to the difficulty of obtaining decisions in groups with members holding widely different views?

10. How is *lateral thinking* likely to help avoid some of the difficulties of data gathering prior to a decision?

11. What is the likely value of the tactic of reversing situations in order to explore the original situations fully?

12. How can the leader of a data gathering enquiry ensure that the opinions and views he obtains are not drawn from only one stream? What can be done to change the methods of enquiry once investigation has been started?

13. Is incrementalism just another name for conservatism? Are there situations that you have experienced where a radical or innovative course of action failed? Do you suspect that an incremental measure might have succeeded?

14. Are incremental courses of action necessarily remedial, or can they result in long-term solutions to problems?

15. Are fundamental decisions usually seen to be made incorrectly in the light of future events and information? If so, what can be

done to correct this? If not, can you give examples of good fundamental decisions and bad ones and provide reasons for the difference and for your judgements?

16. How would you go about eliminating alternatives at the various levels of the mixed scanning process? Could you incorporate your suggestions into a prescriptive model for use by others?

17. Do people necessarily react negatively to innovative measures or proposals? Under what circumstances might they welcome them? Do some people propose such measures without consideration of possible adverse consequences?

18. Can you give an example of a fundamental decision preceded and followed by a series of incremental ones? If so, what precipitated the fundamental decision and why were the others only incremental?

19. How is stress likely to affect the performance of an individual involved in the resolution of a complex decision problem? If any of the effects you describe are considered undesirable, how would you go about reducing the possibility of their occurrence?

20. If you were the leader of a group involved in decision making, would you introduce some stress and tension into the group in order to improve performance? If so, how would you do it and how would you ensure that it did not get out of hand?

## REFERENCES

1. Martino, Joseph P. *Technological Forecasting for Decision Making.* New York: American Elsevier Publishing Co., 1972.

2. Ayres, Robert U. *Technological Forecasting and Long-Range Planning.* New York: McGraw-Hill, 1969.

3. Gordon, T. J., and O. Hayward. "Initial Experiments with the Cross Impact Matrix Method of Forecasting." *Futures* 1 (1968): 100–106.

4. Enzer, Selwyn. "Delphi and Cross Impact Techniques." *Futures* 3 (1971): 48–61.

5. Martino, J. P. *Technological Forecasting*, op. cit., pp. 19–20.

6. Gordon, T. J., and O. Helmer. "Report on a Long-Range Forecasting Study." *Rand Corporation Report* P-2982, 1964.

7. Heiss, K. P., K. Knorr, and O. Morgenstern. *Long Term Projections of Power.* Cambridge, Mass.: Ballinger Publishing Co., 1973, pp. 16–26.

8. Turoff, M. "Delphi and Its Potential Impact on Information Systems." AFIPS–Conference Proceedings, vol. 39. Montvale, N.J.: AFIPS Press.

9. Delbecq, A. L., A. H. Ven, and D. H. Gustafson. *Group Techniques for Program Planning.* Glenview, Ill.: Scott, Foresman and Company, 1975, pp. 88–107.

10. Martino, J. P. *Technological Forecasting*, op. cit., pp. 20–64.
11. Lindblom, C. E. "The Science of Muddling Through." *Public Administration Review* 19 (Spring, 1959). Reprinted in *Readings on Modern Organizations*, edited by A. Etzioni. Englewood Cliffs, N.J.: Prentice-Hall, Inc., 1964, pp. 154–73.
12. Braybrooke, D., and C. E. Lindblom. *A Strategy of Decision*. New York: Basic Books, 1963.
13. Dror, Y. "Muddling Through: Science or Inertia." *Public Administration Review* 24 (Sept. 1964).
14. Dror, Y. *Public Policymaking Re-Examined*. New York: Chandler Publishing Co., 1968, pp. 145–6.
15. Etzioni, A. "Mixed Scanning: A 'Third' Approach to Decision Making." *Public Administration Review* 27 (Dec. 1967): 385–92.
16. Braybrooke, D., and C. E. Lindblom. *A Strategy of Decision*, op. cit., p. 79.
17. Etzioni, A. *The Active Society*, New York: Free Press, 1968, Chapter 12 (paperback ed.).
18. Simon, Herbert A. *Administrative Behavior*. New York: The Free Press, 1965, p. xxv (paperback ed.).
19. Etzioni, A. *The Active Society*, op. cit., p. 287.
20. Braybrooke, D., and C. E. Lindblom. *A Strategy of Decision*. New York: The Free Press, pp. 83–88.
21. Etzioni, A. "Mixed Scanning," op. cit., p. 388.
22. Easton, Allan. *Complex Managerial Decisions Involving Multiple Objectives*. New York: John Wiley & Sons, 1973.
23. MacCrimmon, Kenneth R. "An Overview of Multiple Objective Decision Making." In *Multiple Criteria Decision Making*, edited by J. L. Cochrane, and M. Zeleny. Columbia, S.C.: University of South Carolina Press, 1973, pp. 18–44.
24. A more detailed discussion of goal programming (and a practical example) is given in Sang M. Lee. "Goal Programming for Decision Analysis of Multiple Objectives." *Sloan Management Review*, Winter, 1972, pp. 11–24.
25. MacCrimmon, K. R. "Multiple Objective Decision Making," op. cit., pp. 30–33.
26. Adams, James L. *Conceptual Blockbusting: A Guide to Better Ideas*. San Francisco: W. H. Freeman and Company, 1974.
27. Ibid., Chapters 5, 6 and 7.
28. de Bono, Edward. *Lateral Thinking*. London: Ward Lock Educational Ltd., 1970.
29. Milburn, T. W. "The Management of Crises." In *International Crises: Insights from Behavioral Research*, edited by G. F. Herman. New York: The Free Press, 1972, pp. 259–77.
30. Ibid., p. 265.
31. Lanzetta, J. T. "Group Behavior Under Stress." In *Human Behavior and International Politics: Contributions from the Social-Psychological*

*Sciences*, edited by J. D. Singer. Skokie, Ill.: Rand McNally & Company, 1965, p. 216–17.

32. Hamblin, R. L. "Group Integration During a Crisis." In *Human Behavior*, J. D. Singer, ed., op. cit., pp. 226–28.

33. Pruitt, D. G. "Definition of the Situation as a Determinant of International Action." In *International Behavior: A Social-Psychological Analysis*, edited by H. C. Kelman. New York: Holt, Rinehart and Winston, 1965, pp. 395–96.

34. For some examples of these miscalculations, see:
    Smith, Richard Austen. *Corporations in Crisis*. New York: Doubleday Anchor paperbacks, A475, 1964;
    Ryan, Cornelius. *A Bridge too Far*. New York: Simon and Schuster, 1974;
    Fall, Bernard B. *Hell in a Very Small Place—The Siege of Dien Bien Phu*. Philadelphia, Pa.: J. B. Lippincott Company, 1966;
    Stoessinger, John G. *Why Nations Go to War*. New York: St. Martins Press, 1974.

35. Janis, Irving L. *Victims of Group-Think*. Boston, Mass.: Houghton Mifflin Company, 1972.

36. Ibid., p. 9.

37. Arrow, K. J. *Social Choice and Individual Values*, 2d ed. Cowles Foundation Monograph, No. 12, Yale University, 1963. (Originally published by John Wiley & Sons, 1951), pp. 22–23.

38. Janis, I. L. *Victims of Group-Think*, op. cit., pp. 209–19.

# 4

# Analysis of the Strategic Structure of the Problem

In most complex decision problems the interests of the participants are in some degree of conflict. This conflict may be due to the participants having different perceptions of the problem, different objectives, different value systems, or a combination of all of these. The result of this conflict is that participants may have different preferences among the available alternatives and may each wish to bring about a future situation that is incompatible with the desires of the others.

Resolution of complex decision problems in which such conflict exists cannot be accomplished unilaterally by any one of the participants. Attempts by one participant to bring about a resolution based only on his own interests (and neglecting those of others with power to influence the outcome) usually results only in instability. It may also result in escalation of the conflict. A process of resolution of the problem more likely to bring about a stable outcome is one in which the interaction of participants' preferences for possible future scenarios is considered by all concerned. In this way an outcome that is jointly acceptable to the participants can be sought. Such an outcome is not likely to provide each participant with the alternative that he prefers most. However, it may be a better outcome than he could achieve by a unilateral process of decision insomuch as it is more likely to be stable.

It is interesting to note that in the search for jointly acceptable

74

outcomes, conflict and cooperation are intimately linked together. The existence of conflict promotes cooperation by giving rise to the need for it. There is ample evidence of this phenomenon in the everyday affairs of organizations in modern society and business. These organizations do not usually battle with one another to the point where one or the other is totally defeated. Nor are these organizations able to pursue what they perceive as their optimum courses of action regardless of the existence and wishes of others in their area of operation. They can obtain an acceptable measure of attainment of their objectives only by cooperating openly or implicitly with others. In such cases, each participant may not achieve all his objectives, but each attains more by cooperation than would otherwise be the case. Conflict is therefore often a means of achieving some kind of unity. It may in many instances be an integrative rather than a destructive force in social and business affairs.[1]

In the second phase of the process of resolution of complex decision problems, the interaction of the participants' preferences for courses of action and future scenarios is considered. The analysis of that interaction leads to an appreciation of the strategic structure of the problem. This is a necessary preliminary to the process of negotiation and bargaining between the participants that determines which of a number of jointly acceptable outcomes is in fact adopted by them.

The same two temporary simplifications adopted in the previous chapter will be used again in examining the second phase of the process of resolution. The interaction between the participants will be discussed primarily from the point of view of one participant. It will not be forgotten, however, that this one participant's perception of the intentions, attitudes, and preferences of the others is not necessarily correct. This possible error must ultimately be allowed for in any proposed procedure for dealing with complex problems. Also, the second phase will be examined (as was the case with the first) by temporarily stopping the flow of time. Most of the discussion in this chapter will therefore be of the situation in one "time slice". The dynamic nature of complex decision problems will be reintroduced in the discussion of an overall procedure for resolution treated in a later section of the text.

## ANALYTICAL TREATMENTS OF
## SITUATIONS INVOLVING CONFLICT

One of the earliest analytical treatments of conflict was that of Lewis F. Richardson. Working in the period 1920–1950, Richardson collected statistics on many aspects of war and incorporated them into a "theory of arms races."[2, 3] In its simplest form this theory provides a mathematical relationship between parameters in models representing the armaments programs of two competing countries. As in many other instances of scientific inquiry, study of this simplified model provided insights into more complex real-life situations. Richardson was able to show, under the conditions of his simplified model, that a point of balance of power might exist in an arms race and that the location of this balance point would depend on the values assigned to factors that defined the overall situation. Furthermore, he suggested that the balance could be called stable, unstable, or neutral according to the behavior of the system after it had been disturbed by some temporary external influence. More complex versions of the Richardson model allow consideration of constraints or system boundaries that may prevent a balance point being reached under certain conditions. The effect of these constraints might be to induce a change in the conflict situation (or in its boundaries) such that a desired balance position can, in fact, be reached.

Later analytical approaches to conflict situations, under the general heading of game theory, are concerned with models of these situations constructed in terms of:[4]

- *participants* (or *players*) involved in the conflict situation;
- *options, available courses of action, policies,* or *strategies* of these participants;
- *outcomes* resulting from choices of strategies by the participants;
- *preferences* of the participants for these outcomes.

Each participant in the decision situation (or game) wishes to bring about an outcome that he judges is best for him or that is at least high on his scale of preferences. If he could bring about such an outcome by a unilateral choice from among his available options, his problem would be relatively simple. However, in a conflict situation, the outcome is dependent not only on his own preferences between options but also upon those of the other participants.

One of the main features in the treatment of complex decision problems by means of game theoretic models is the study of choices of strategies that can result in an *equilibrium*. An equilibrium in game theory is defined as a situation brought about by a choice of options by the players, from which it is not advantageous for any of the players to move, *provided that none of the players do move*. All game situations have at least one equilibrium of one sort or another.

The existence of equilibria in a conflict situation provides the participants with promise of a measure of stability that may allow them to avoid the worst of the possible outcomes at the expense of not achieving the best.

The difficulty experienced by all participants in conflict situations is that information on the choices of options by those involved is usually kept secret, at least until someone sees possible advantage in revealing his plans. Even when such revelations are made, there is usually uncertainty as to whether the information divulged is true and complete, or whether some degree of bluffing is included. The result may therefore be that participants in such situations make cautious and exploratory moves designed more to gain information about the others' intentions than to resolve the problem in which they are all engaged. If, however, the choices of options of each participant were revealed to all the others, it might be possible for them to examine a number of outcomes that they could bring about by *coordinated* choices of options. One or more of these outcomes might be judged by all participants to be preferable to the situation in which there was no coordinated choice and a consequent continuation of the conflict.

It is, of course, unlikely that participants in a real-life situation would suddenly agree to reveal their plans and intentions to all the others involved (although it is often suggested that each should do so confidentially to a mediator in order to resolve a particularly difficult problem). However, the unlikelihood of complete disclosure of intentions in practical circumstances should not prevent us from studying the situation that would arise if one participant were to know the intentions of all the others. There might, in fact, be considerable advantage to a participant who carried out such a study based on his best estimates of all the options available to the others involved and their preferences for outcomes. This advantage would arise from the broader view of the decision situation that would be obtained, the knowledge of possible outcomes that might arise from particular choices of options by the participants and the ability to react to such choices from a basis of previous study.

## Metagames

The opportunity to obtain this broader view of a complex decision problem in which participants with conflicting interests are involved arises in the study of metagames.[5] In carrying out such a study, the decision situation is considered as a game. The participants and the options that are considered to be feasible and available to each of them are listed after consideration of the elements of the situation described in Chapter 2 of this text. A metagame is a hypothetical situation that would arise if a particular participant (player) knew the choices of options and strategies of each of the others involved. By studying a number of these metagames, it is possible to explore what might transpire in the original situation if the strategy choices of the participants in that situation were made clear to the others involved. In particular, outcomes (called meta-equilibria) might be discovered that do not appear as equilibria in the original game situation, but that actually result from the participants' knowledge of each others' choices of options and preferences.[6] If such a meta-equilibrium exists, it may be a position to which the players would wish to move, once the existence of such a possibility is made known to them. It is precisely this type of search for a mutually profitable resolution of a situation involving conflicting interests that occurs in practice prior to the signing of a contract, treaty, or agreement between the participants.

It must be said immediately that the existence of a metaequilibrium does not necessarily indicate the solution to a decision problem in which conflict between the interests of the participants is involved. A metaequilibrium is rather a position that can be jointly sought by participants who wish to obtain some stability in a conflict situation. Adoption of strategies leading to a metaequilibrium is therefore a result of decision making behavior in a conflict situation rather than representing a uniquely rational solution to the problems arising in that situation. In many respects, it is analogous to the strategy of uncertainty avoidance in conditions of limited information about future natural events. In an actual decision situation, the choice of options depends on the attitudes and behavioral characteristics of all the participants. One or more of the participants may not regard a condition of stability as being in his short or long-term interests. He may choose, therefore, to move away from the equilibrium position, rather than towards it, and hope to induce others to do so also. By this means, he may be able to create an outcome that is more advantageous for himself.

The metagames derived from any particular decision situation may contain more than one metaequilibrium and if this is the case, any two different metaequilibria may represent different outcomes of the decision situation. The relative benefits to any participants arising from these different metaequilibria may be substantially different. In these circumstances, therefore, there may be contention and disagreement over which of the metaequilibria should be chosen as the basis for a stable resolution of the conflict situation. Furthermore, by definition one participant cannot advantageously leave an equilibrium if the others remain. Movement from one metaequilibrium position to another can therefore be achieved only by mutual consent of the participants. The question of which metaequilibrium of the many that may exist should be chosen as the basis of an agreement is often the subject of much negotiation and bargaining. It is this question that is most often at the root of industrial relations disputes in which a number of possible solutions exist, some more to the advantage of management and some more to the benefit of labor.

## THE ANALYSIS OF OPTIONS

The practical approach to complex decision problems based on the study of metagames is known as the *analysis of options* or *metagame analysis*.[7, 8] When using this technique, the complex decision problem to be analyzed is viewed as a game situation and the analysis procedure is the equivalent of reviewing the metagames derived from this game situation. In essence, the analysis provides a method of determining which of the present or possible future scenarios can be regarded as metaequilibria and which may, therefore, offer grounds for a stable resolution of the problem situation for the participants. The analysis is not solely concerned with equilibria. If a particular scenario is analyzed and found not to be a metaequilibrium, it may be concluded that one or more of the participants could move away from that scenario and thereby obtain an improvement in his position. The analysis usually (but not necessarily) starts with consideration of the present situation. It then provides for a review of a range of possible future scenarios taking into account all the participants and the best available information on their options and their preferences for outcomes.

The first step in using the analysis of options technique is to list the participants in the decision situation and the possible courses of action or options open to each of them. Each participant normally has a number of options, each of which he can choose to implement or not. A statement of intent indicating whether or not a participant will implement each of his options is usually called his *strategy*. Combinations of the strategies of all the participants represent *scenarios*, as discussed earlier in the text.

Suppose, for the purpose of illustration, that one of the participants involved in a complex decision problem wishes to assess a particular scenario and to determine whether that scenario could be expected to be stable as a result of some implicit or explicit agreement between all concerned. The particular scenario chosen for analysis might be the existing situation or, equally well, a situation that would result from some or all of the participants implementing some of their available options. The analysis is concerned first with determining whether or not the particular scenario under consideration is a meta-equilibrium; that is, whether or not it would be stable when the strategy choices of each of the participants are known to all the others. Since a scenario is stable only if it is stable for each participant separately, the stability of the particular scenario under consideration must be investigated for each participant in turn. The stability of the particular scenario for a particular participant will be questionable only if there exists a strategy by which he can improve his position by acting unilaterally, assuming, for the moment, that the strategies of the others involved remain unchanged. The situation resulting from such a change of strategy is called a *unilateral improvement* for him.

To determine whether a unilateral improvement exists for any particular participant, the strategy choices of that participant are varied while keeping those of the others fixed. Each new scenario thus created is examined to determine whether it is *preferred* or *not preferred* by the particular participant, as compared to the particular scenario originally chosen for analysis. A preferred scenario is a unilateral improvement, since it can be brought about by unilateral action on the part of the particular participant. If no unilateral improvement can be found, the original scenario can be considered as stable for the participant concerned, provided that he believes that the others will maintain their stated positions. It is logical for the participant to remain at this stable position in these circumstances (at least for the time being), since he has no means of improving his position by an action on his part. If no unilateral improvement can be found for any participant after repeating the analysis for each of them, the particular scenario under consideration is stable for all participants. The position can, therefore, be considered to be an equilibrium at which the participants may wish to stay pending any future developments.

It is important to recall at this stage that information concerning the options and preferences of the participants used in the analysis are only the best estimates of those doing the work. They are usually based on careful scrutiny and consideration of the elements of the decision situation described in Chapter 2, as they apply to each of the participants to whom the preferences are attributed. However, these preferences cannot be known exactly by the participant undertaking the analysis. It is important, therefore, that those drawing conclusions take account of any variation in the preferences of the participants and changes in any other important factors. The sensitivity of the conclusions to such changes should be checked from time to time during the analysis. The manner in which this can be done is discussed in a later section of this chapter devoted to sensitivity testing.

To continue the description of the analysis of options method in its simplest form, let us assume that a unilateral improvement has been found for one particular participant. It is now necessary to consider what actions on the part of the other participants might deter him from taking advantage of the improvement. Note that a decision as to whether or not he would actually be deterred from taking the improvement would depend on his beliefs concerning whether or not the other participant would in fact take these actions. Any such action by any one or more of the other participants is called a *sanction* against the participant having the available unilateral improvement. It is necessary in the course of the analysis to consider all possible sanctions against the particular participant by the others, relative to the particular scenario being considered. This is done by varying the available options of the other participants and deciding for each combination of their options whether the new scenario represented by each such combination is preferred or not preferred by the original participant, whatever course of action he takes. If a particular combination of the other participants' available options is not preferred whatever the particular participant does, this is a sanction against him. This procedure is repeated until all sanctions have been found. The scenario being considered is then said to be stable for the particular participant, as long as he believes that, if he were to take one of his unilateral improvements, the others would react by implementing a sanction. If, however, no sanctions exist against the particular participant being considered, a further step is indicated. This further step consists of looking for all *inescapable* (or *guaranteed*) *improvements* for the participant from the particular scenario being considered. Such an improvement is better for him whatever the others may do in terms of choosing from their stated available options.

The procedure described in the preceding paragraphs can be formalized into a series of steps as follows:

*Step 1.* List all the participants involved in the decision situation and all their available options.

*Step 2.* List details of the particular scenario to be evaluated. This is done in terms of the options of the participants in that scenario. The particular scenario chosen need not be the current situation (status quo), although it might be. The general question to be answered is "What if we were in this particular situation: would it be stable?"

*Step 3.* Select a particular participant (or coalition) with respect to whom it is desired to evaluate the stability of a particular scenario made up of potential choices of available options by the participants in the decision situation;

*Step 4.* Find all the unilateral improvements from the particular scenario for the participant or coalition selected. If none exists, proceed to assess the unilateral improvements available to all other participants and coalitions in turn (that is, return to Step 3). If a unilateral improvement exists for the particular participant or coalition proceed to Step 5. (Some combinations of options may be judged infeasible and can be neglected at this stage.)

*Step 5.* Determine all the sanctions available to the other participants against the particular participant or coalition relative to the particular scenario (Neglect infeasibilities). If a sanction exists against the particular participant return to Step 2 or Step 3 and consider any other scenario, participants, or coalition of participants. If no sanction exists, proceed to Step 6.

*Step 6.* Find all inescapable (or guaranteed) improvements for the particular participant or coalition from the particular scenario. Return to Step 1 to consider different sets of options, to Step 2 to consider a different particular scenario, or to Step 3 to consider a different particular participant or coalition.

This procedure is shown in the form of a flow chart in Figure 4.1. In practical applications of the analysis, the procedure is repeated for all participants, for all important potential coalitions of participants, and for a number of possible scenarios.

### An Example of the Analysis of Options

As an example of the application of the analysis of options, let us consider in more detail the situation described in Chapter 3 under the heading "The Construction of Facility X." The participants and options in this situation were developed in that chapter and are shown again for convenient reference in Table 4.1. The following is a

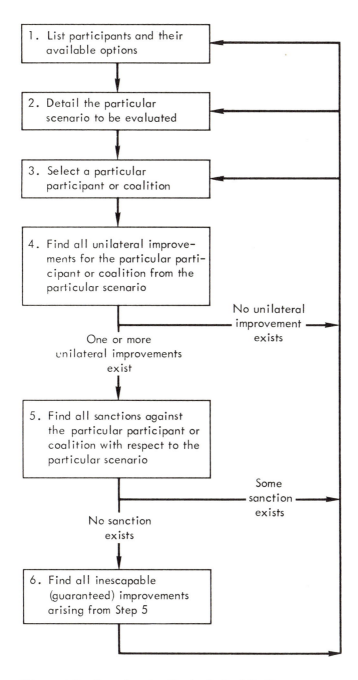

1. List participants and their available options

2. Detail the particular scenario to be evaluated

3. Select a particular participant or coalition

4. Find all unilateral improvements for the particular participant or coalition from the particular scenario

No unilateral improvement exists

One or more unilateral improvements exist

5. Find all sanctions against the particular participant or coalition with respect to the particular scenario

Some sanction exists

No sanction exists

6. Find all inescapable (guaranteed) improvements arising from Step 5

Figure 4.1 *Procedure for the Analysis of Options*

83

more detailed description of the background of this hypothetical decision problem.

A large organization has decided that it must construct a major facility at "Site A." It has formed a Project Group to supervise the planning and construction of the facility. The facility can be thought of as a nuclear power station, a refinery or chemical plant, a factory, an airport, or even a freeway. The facility is necessary to meet the demand for services or products. However, it has certain disadvantages in terms of possible pollution of the atmosphere and the environment; danger of explosion or leakage of noxious gases and materials; spoliation of farmland, recreation land, and natural beauty of the countryside; and disruption of the life-style and daily routine of the local inhabitants. The degree to which any of these factors is a major hazard to the surrounding countryside and to its residents is unknown. A number of estimates of the effect of these factors has been produced and the validity of the information on which they are based is a subject of dispute at the time of the analysis.

Opposition to the location of the facility at Site A has been mounting. An organization has been formed called Citizens' Protest to concentrate this opposition. It plans to take any necessary steps to stop construction or, at least, to force modification of plans for the facility to make it more acceptable to the residents of the area. Citizens' Protest wants present plans for construction at the site to be abandoned in favor of a proposal to build a much smaller facility. They favor this over complete opposition to any sort of facility because of the money and continuing employment that the development will bring into the area. The movement has initiated action to delay construction, including persuading some local tradesmen and businesses to refuse to service or supply the site. These measures are reinforced by a program of picketing and minor civil disobedience as an additional means of establishing bargaining power in any future negotiations. Political parties in opposition to the government have offered support to the Citizens' Protest movement, possibly with a view to unseating the local elected members (who support the government) and replacing the government in power at the upcoming election.

Citizens' Protest has consulted a group of knowledgeable individuals who have proposed a compromise in which a mid-size facility would be built with adequate precautions observed to ensure safety and protection of the environment and ecology.

Two other participants are in supporting roles. Local elected representatives are in the predicament of wishing to support the majority view of citizens in their constituency, of being subject to the influence

Table 4.1   PARTICIPANTS AND OPTIONS IN THE "CONSTRUCTION OF
FACILITY X" DISPUTE

| Participants | Options | Present Scenario (Read Down) | Proposed Compromise (Read Down) | Infeasibles | |
|---|---|---|---|---|---|
| Project Group | Continue construction of large facility | 1 | 0 | 1 | 1 |
| | Build small facility at Site A | 0 | 0 | 1 | 1 |
| | Settle for mid-size facility | 0 | 1 | 1 | 1 |
| Citizens' Protest | Support Government in election | 1 | 1 | | |
| | Picket construction site | 1 | 0 | | |
| | Settle for mid-size facility | 0 | 1 | | 1 |
| Elected Representatives | Support Citizens' Protest | 1 | 1 | | 1 |
| Government | Provide support to Project Group | 1 | 1 | | |
| Nature | Recession | 0 | | | |
| | Disaster | 0 | | | |
| | Technological development | 0 | | | |

85

of the political party that they represent, and also of acting according to their own information about the hazards and benefits of the project. The local representatives' dilemma is shown in simplified form as the option to support (or not) the Citizens' Protest Group. The government with jurisdiction over the project is also a participant because it must authorize the installation, provide support, and administer any funding for the facility.

The effect of natural or quasi-natural uncertainty on the decision problem is introduced by showing an additional participant called *Nature* and representative possible options of Nature as *Recession, Disaster* and *Technological Development.* These options are meant to represent; (a) the possibility that recession in the economy will cause the demand for the product or service to be less than that estimated in the original planning of the facility; (b) the chance that a disaster at a similar facility elsewhere will affect views, opinions, value systems and ultimately preferences for scenarios; and (c) the possibility that future technological developments will make possible a smaller, safer, or less unsightly facility.

The Project Group views the situation as one in which it has three options:

1. to continue construction of the large facility at Site A with a view to keeping open for as long as possible the option of a large facility. This would involve additional expense because certain labor and services would need to be brought in from other areas to replace those that are temporarily unavailable locally;

2. to accede to the Citizens' Protest demands that a small facility be built at the site; and

3. to negotiate in the hope of arriving at a settlement involving a mid-size facility.

Moving construction to another site is not regarded as an available option at the present time because of the amount already invested in Site A. Much of that investment would be applicable to construction of a mid-size facility at that site, but very little of the work already completed could be used if only a small facility were to be built. Furthermore, work can continue for a while at the site without major loss if the eventual decision is to change to a mid-size facility.

### Details of the Analysis

The following description is indicative of how the problem situation just outlined might be analyzed by one of the participants, say the Project Group. The analysis follows the steps illustrated in Figure 4.1 and the description is continued through some (but not all) of the possible iterations indicated·in the flow diagram. Complete documentation of an analysis of this sort is lengthy and often somewhat repetitious. For this reason, only sufficient detail is presented here to allow the reader to form an impression of the nature of the analysis. Those requiring more detail of an analysis of this sort are referred to other published accounts of the technique.[9, 10, 11, 12] Those who find reading of the tables tedious can instead follow the text in this and the following section and find the analysis summarized in Figures 4.2 and 4.3 and in the description accompanying these diagrams.

Let us suppose at the outset that the Project Group wishes to examine the stability of the proposed compromise (shown in Table 4.1) in which the two major protagonists settle for a mid-sized facility with the respective support of the other participants in the situation. The technique of analysis requires that this scenario be examined for stability with respect to each participant in turn. This is done by making an assessment of whether each participant has one or more unilateral improvements from the scenario that are not offset by credible sanctions capable of being invoked by other participants or coalitions of participants. If no credible sanction exists, the improvement is inescapable or guaranteed for the particular participant and the conclusion is that the scenario under consideration is not likely to be stable.

The analysis is carried out by considering all the scenarios that can be constructed from the options of the particular participant (the Project Group) and making a judgement whether (all possible actions by the other participant being ignored for the present) each feasible new scenario would be "preferred" or "not preferred" by the Project Group to the particular scenario (the proposed compromise) being considered. This phase of the analysis is illustrated in Table 4.2. Note that because there are three options shown against the Project Group, each of which this participant can elect to implement or not, there are eight ($2^3$) possible scenarios. One of these is the proposed compromise. Of the other seven, three are shown as "preferred," one as "not preferred," and three are infeasible. It is important in conducting the analysis that all possible scenarios resulting from combinations of the participant's options are considered, lest a potential unilateral improvement that might disrupt stability be overlooked. Note again at this time that the judgement as to whether a scenario is preferred or not preferred is made to the best of the ability of the individual or team conducting the analysis and that this judgement may not be accurate. However, pending later consideration of this aspect, let us

Table 4.2   UNILATERAL IMPROVEMENTS FROM THE PROPOSED COMPROMISE FOR THE PROJECT GROUP

| Participants | Options | Preferred by Project Group | | | Proposed Compromise | Not Preferred by Project Group | Infeasible | | | |
|---|---|---|---|---|---|---|---|---|---|---|
| Project Group | Continue construction of large facility | 1 | 1 | 0 | 0 | 0 | | | 1 | 1 |
| | Build small facility at Site A | 0 | 0 | 0 | 0 | 1 | | | 1 | 1 |
| | Settle for mid-size facility | 0 | 1 | 0 | 1 | 0 | | | 1 | 1 |
| Citizens' Protest | Support Government in election | | | | 1 | | | | | |
| | Picket construction site | | | | 0 | | | | | |
| | Settle for mid-size facility | | | | 1 | | | | | |
| Elected Representatives | Support citizens' protest | | | | 1 | | | | | |
| Government | Provide support to project group | | | | 1 | | | | | |
| | Column number | 1 | 2 | 3 | 4 | 5 | 6 | 7 | 8 | 9 |

Three different unilateral improvements

suppose for the moment that judgements of this nature are made accurately.

The unilateral improvements shown in Table 4.2 indicate that the Project Group is judged to prefer to continue construction of the large facility to immediate settlement at the compromise position, whether or not it finally has to settle for the mid-size facility (Columns 1 and 2). Furthermore, it prefers not to settle at the present time, whether or not it is prevented from continuing present construction of the large facility (Columns 1 and 3). The alternative of building a small facility (as demanded by Citizens' Protest) is not preferred to the proposed compromise, as indicated in Column 5. The remaining scenarios arising from the Project Groups' options are judged to be infeasible (Columns 6, 7, and 8). These judgements are shown in a modified format in Table 4.3 where a dash is taken to mean "whether or not." This modification allows a number of scenarios to be represented in a single column, with a consequent saving of space in the table. In a further refinement, figures are shown in Table 4.3 in the "preferred" columns to denote the *worst* of the two alternatives denoted by the dash. This notation provides considerable economy in representing scenarios, since if the *worst* of a set of alternatives is preferred, clearly all the others would be more preferred and need not be considered in detail at this stage of the analysis. In the "not preferred" column, the figure indicates the *best* of the alternatives, since if the *best* is not preferred, clearly the others would be even less preferred.

The next step is to consider whether any action by another participant (or combination of actions by other participants) would represent a sanction against the Project Group. If a potential sanction exists and if the Project Group really believes that the other participants could and would exercise it to prevent the Group from moving away from the possible compromise (that is, if the potential sanction is judged to be *credible* to the Project Group) the effect of the sanction would be to add stability to the compromise solution. If no credible sanction exists, the compromise is not a basis for stable resolution of the problem.

A simple example of a sanction against the Project Group is shown in Column 3 of Table 4.4. It consists of a withdrawal of support by the government. Note that in the judgement of the individual or team conducting the analysis this withdrawal of support makes all scenarios containing it "not preferred" by the Project Group to the compromise. The power of this sanction by the government is shown by the fact that if support is not withdrawn (Column 1 in Table 4.4),

Table 4.3  MODIFIED FORMAT FOR SHOWING UNILATERAL IMPROVEMENTS

| Participants | Options | Preferred by Project Group | | Proposed Compromise | Not Preferred by Project Group | Infeasible | | |
|---|---|---|---|---|---|---|---|---|
| Project Group | Continue construction of large facility | 1 | 1 | 0 | 0 | 0 | 1 | 1 |
| | Build small facility at Site A | 0 | 0 | 0 | 1 | 1 | 1 | 1 |
| | Settle for mid-size facility | 0 | 1 | 1 | 0 | 1 | 0 | 1 |

*may be written as*

| Participants | Options | Preferred by Project Group | | Proposed Compromise | Not Preferred by Project Group | Infeasible | |
|---|---|---|---|---|---|---|---|
| Project Group | Continue construction of large facility | 1 | –(0) | 0 | 0 | – | 1 |
| | Build small facility at Site A | 0 | 0 | 0 | 1 | 1 | 1 |
| | Settle for mid-size facility | –(1) | 0 | 1 | 0 | 1 | 0 |

where the dash (thus "–") means "whether or not" or "1 or 0." This allows two or more columns to be shown in one.

NOTE: The figure in brackets thus, (1) in the "preferred" column denotes the *worst* of the alternatives. (In the not preferred column, it would show the *best*.)

the Project Group prefers to continue construction of the large facility for the time being, whatever the other participants may do.

It may be asked, legitimately, what has been gained by the analysis so far? The main benefit is in the orderly arrangement and display of possible future scenarios and in the introduction of the estimated preferences of the participants for those scenarios into a structured analysis. The tables constructed to this point contain no new information and there is no sudden emergence of a solution in a manner that many have become accustomed to expect from quantitative analysis. However, the tables do provide some insurance that no combination of anticipated actions by the participants is overlooked. In addition, they allow explicit consideration of the interaction between the participants in a complex decision situation, taking into account their estimated preferences for possible scenarios.

The conclusions thus far in our simple example are that there are three unilateral improvements from the proposed compromise for the Project Group, but that these improvements would be negated by Government withdrawing support from the Project Group. The possibility of withdrawal of this support would therefore be a powerful influence toward making the proposed compromise stable and a meaningful basis for agreement. It would now be necessary in a full analysis to repeat the procedure to determine whether any other participant could bring about unilateral improvements from the proposed compromise and whether any credible sanctions existed. Let us suppose that this has been done, that no improvements were found for individual participants, and that, therefore, no sanctions needed to be considered. The situation at this point can be illustrated by the diagram shown in Figure 4.2. This shows the three unilateral improvements found for the Project Group from the Proposed Compromise and the sanction by Government against those improvements. Implementation of the sanction leads to a situation called *no funding or support by Government* in which no one participant (apart possibly from the Elected Representatives) has achieved a situation as beneficial to them as the proposed compromise. Project Group has no Government support and therefore probably can make only limited future progress in construction of a facility of any sort. Citizens' Protest has little money entering the area as a result of the construction stoppage and Government has no progress toward a needed facility. The question now arises of what the participants can do next. Project Group is aware of the key question of government support and decides to investigate a possible coalition with Government with the aim of preventing the withdrawal of support.

Possible unilateral improvements of a coalition of Project Group

Table 4.4 A Sanction Against the Project Group with Respect to the Proposed Compromise

| Participants | Options | Preferred by Project Group | Proposed Compromise | Not Preferred by Project Group |
|---|---|---|---|---|
| Project Group | Continue construction of large facility | 1 | 0 | -(1) |
| | Build small facility at Site A | 0 | 0 | -(0) |
| | Settle for mid-size facility | 0 | 1 | -(0) |
| Citizens' Protest | Support Government in election | -(1) | 1 | -(0) |
| | Picket construction site | -(1) | 0 | -(0) |
| | Settle for mid-size facility | -(0) | 1 | -(0) |
| Elected Representatives | Support Citizens' Protest | -(1) | 1 | -(0) |
| Government | Provide support to Project Group | 1 | 1 | 0 |
| | Column number | 1 | 2 | 3 |

Still preferred as long as Government provides funding ↑ (column 1)

Sanction by Government ↑ (column 3)

NOTE: Infeasibles (same as Table 4.2) omitted.

92

and Government from the proposed compromise are investigated first. In the judgement of the analysis team, two situations are better than the proposed compromise for the coalition. These are shown in Columns 1 and 2 of Table 4.5. Column 1 represents a situation in which Project Group continues with present construction leaving open the possibility of a large facility at some future time, whether or not it eventually settles for the mid-size facility. Column 2 is the situation in which Project Group holds out for a large facility whether or not it continues construction at the present time. Note that the figures in parentheses in the preferred column in this Table are different for Project Group and Government, denoting that although the coalition prefers the situation described by the column, different variants of it are least preferred by individual members of the coalition.

Having determined that unilateral improvements exist for the coalition, it is now necessary to investigate possible sanctions against the coalition by other participants. One such sanction might be action by a coalition of Citizens' Protest and Elected Representatives to delay the project. This is shown in Columns 4 and 5 of Table 4.6. The action involved might, for example, be defeat of sitting representatives of the party forming government (or even defeat of the whole government) in an election. The possibility of this action might force Government to withdraw from the Project Group-Government coalition and precipitate a return to the *no funding or support by Government* scenario of Figure 4.2. The situation at this point is illustrated in Figure 4.3. This new diagram is based on the contents of Tables 4.5 and 4.6 and presents conclusions that can be drawn from these Tables in graphic form. Note that the diagram of Figure 4.2 can be joined with that shown in Figure 4.3 to show a comprehensive picture of the analysis so far, but this has not been done here in the interests of simplicity of presentation.

The diagram in Figure 4.3 shows that the unilateral improvements for the Project Group-Government coalition can be negated by a sanction by Citizens' Protest against the Government that we have described as a withdrawal of popular support from the local political representatives or from the government as a whole. This leads to a situation described as *Government loses popular support* shown at the bottom right of the diagram. The analysis could be continued at this point by choosing this situation as the particular scenario and assessing whether any player or coalition had any unilateral or guaranteed improvements from it. A likely conclusion of such analysis is that withdrawal of support and funding from Project Group would be considered to be a unilateral improvement for Government from that scenario. This is shown on the diagram as leading to a situation

Table 4.5  Unilateral Improvements from the Proposed Compromise for a Coalition of Project Group and Government

| Participants | Options | Preferred by Coalition P.G. | Preferred by Coalition Govt. | Proposed Compromise | Not Preferred by Project Group | Not Preferred by Government |
|---|---|---|---|---|---|---|
| Project Group | Continue construction of large facility | 1 | – (0)   (1) | 0 | – (0) | – (0) · |
| | Build small facility at Site A | 0 | 0 | 0 | 1 | – (0) |
| | Settle for mid-size facility | – (1)   (0) | 0 | 1 | – (0) | – (0) |
| Citizens' Protest | Support Government in election | 1 | 1 | 1 | 1 | 1 |
| | Picket construction site | 0 | 0 | 0 | 0 | 0 |
| | Settle for mid-size facility | 1 | 1 | 1 | 1 | 1 |
| Elected Representatives | Support Citizens' Protest | 1 | 1 | 1 | 1 | 1 |
| Government | Provide support to Project Group | 1 | 1 | 1 | – (1) | 0 |
| | Column number | 1 | 2 | 3 | 4 | 5 |

↑
Unilateral improvements for the Project Group–Government Coalition

Table 4.6 SANCTIONS AGAINST THE PROJECT GROUP-GOVERNMENT COALITION WITH RESPECT TO THE PROPOSED COMPROMISE

| Participants | Options | Preferred by Coalition | | | | Proposed Compromise | Not Preferred by | |
|---|---|---|---|---|---|---|---|---|
| | | P.G. | Govt. | P.G. | Govt. | | Project Group | Government |
| Project Group | Continue construction of large facility | 1 | 1 | | | 0 | – (1) | – (1) |
| | Build small facility at Site A | 0 | 0 | | | 0 | 1 | 0 |
| | Settle for mid-size facility | 0 | 0 | | | 1 | – (0) | – (0) |
| Citizens' Protest | Support Government in election | 1 | | – (0) | (0) | 1 | 0 | 0 |
| | Picket construction site | – (1) | (1) | – (1) | (1) | 0 | – (0) | – (0) |
| | Settle for mid-size facility | – (0) | (0) | – (0) | (0) | 1 | – (0) | – (1) |
| Elected Representatives | Support Citizens' Protest | – (1) | (1) | 0 | | 1 | 1 | 1 |
| Government | Provide support to Project Group | 1 | 1 | | | 1 | – (1) | – (1) |
| | Column number | 1 | 2 | | | 3 | 4 | 5 |

↑ Still preferred by Coalition

↑ Sanctions against Project Group–Government Coalition

95

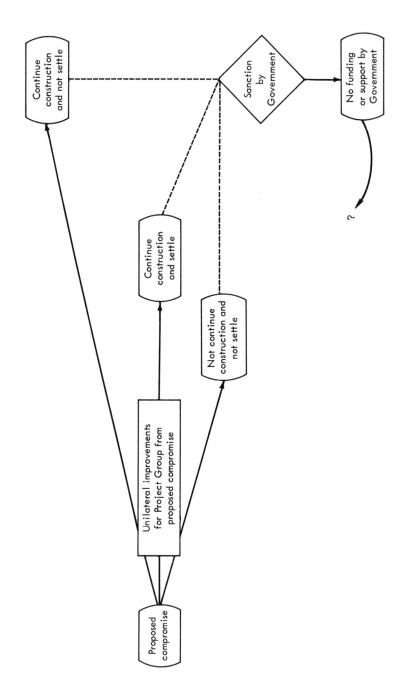

Figure 4.2 Diagram Illustrating First Portion of the Analysis

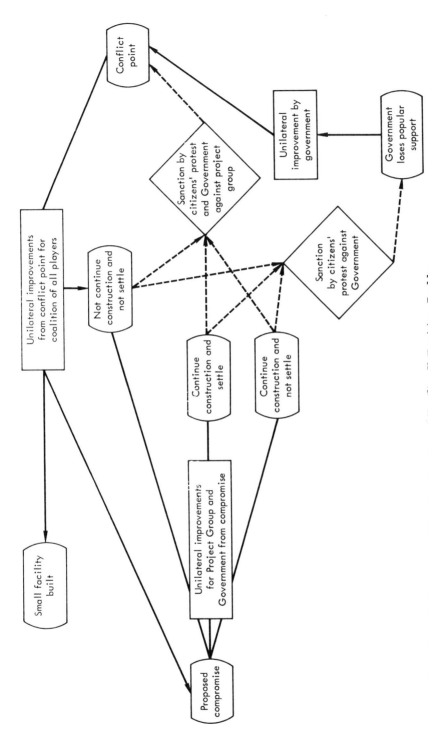

Figure 4.3    *Strategic Structure of the Construction of Facility X Decision Problem*

called *Conflict point*. Note that a sanction by a coalition of Citizens' Protest and Government leads to the same situation.

The conflict point consists of the situation in which all participants are engaged in actions that are not to their individual advantages. It represents a position into which the participants might fall if they were each to carry out actions that they threaten to take as part of the bargaining involved in the decision problem. Specifically, the conflict point in Figure 4.3 consists of the situation shown in Table 4.7:

Table 4.7    THE CONFLICT POINT

| Project Group | Continue construction of large facility | 1 |
| | Build small facility at Site A | 0 |
| | Settle for mid-size facility | 0 |
| Citizens' Protest | Support Government in election | 0 |
| | Picket construction site | 1 |
| | Settle for mid-size facility | 0 |
| Elected Representatives | Support Citizens' Protest | 1 |
| Government | Provide support to Project Group | 0 |

The analysis can now proceed by analyzing the conflict point as the particular scenario and assessing whether any participants or coalitions have any improvements from this scenario. Since the three major participants are all worse off at the conflict point than they might be elsewhere, it is possible that improvements exist for a coalition of these participants. In actual practice, these improvements might come about in a negotiated settlement that provides some improvement for all but is not the most desired situation for each of the participants involved.

Details of this part of the analysis are not given here but they can be derived readily from the preceding Tables. Three situations could result from unilateral improvements from the conflict point for the coalition of the three major participants achieved by negotiation. They are: (a) the original proposed compromise; (b) the situation in which a small facility only is built; and (c) the situation in which the Project Group agrees to halt construction of a large facility in return for some return of support from government. These possible outcomes are shown at the top of Figure 4.3 emanating from the unilateral improvements from the conflict point. The description of the strategic structure of the decision problem as revealed by the analysis so far is completely summarized in that diagram.

It is important to note that the analysis does not predict any outcome or show that any solution is best. It provides instead a description of the possible results of the interaction between the participants based on estimates of their available courses of action and their preferences for scenarios. The actual outcome depends upon a number of factors such as the credibility of the sanction by Citizens' Protest against Government, the willingness of the Project Group to refuse to settle for a mid-size facility in the light of the possibility of loss of support by Government, and the influence that Citizens' Protest can bring to bear to achieve their goal of a small facility.

### INCLUSION OF NATURAL AND
### QUASI-NATURAL EVENTS IN THE ANALYSIS

No account has been taken in the analysis just described of the role of the participant Nature, whose options represent possible natural and quasi-natural events. Since these events are not actions taken in direct opposition to the others involved, Nature cannot be regarded as a full participant in the game. Accordingly, in conducting the analysis, the following conditions are observed: (a) Nature is never selected as the *particular participant;* (b) no preferences are attributed to it; (c) it is never considered to enter into a coalition with another participant; and (d) the procedure of determining unilateral improvements is not applied in the case of the participant Nature. On the other hand, Nature can have an important effect on the analysis as shown in Table 4.8, in which it is seen to have the capability of:

- affecting preferences for an outcome, such as might occur if a favorable technological development made the building of a small facility preferable for all players (Column 1 of Table 4.8).
- imposing the equivalent of a sanction; for example a drop in demand caused by a recession might cause a previously assessed unilateral improvement for Project Group (build a large facility) to be not preferred (Column 3).
- reinforcing the credibility of a sanction, as might happen if a disaster occurred and caused public opinion to support delay of the project (Column 4).
- bringing about an infeasibility; for example, if no technological development occurred a small facility might be infeasible (Column 5).

Table 4.8   INCLUSION OF NATURE IN THE ANALYSIS OF OPTIONS

| Participants | Options | Preferred by Coalition* | Proposed Compromise | Not Preferred by Coalition* | | Infeasible |
|---|---|---|---|---|---|---|
| Project Group | Continue construction of large facility | 0 | 0 | 1 | | |
| | Build small facility at Site A | 1 | 0 | 0 | | 1 |
| | Settle for mid-size facility | 0 | 1 | 0 | | |
| Citizens' Protest | Support Government in election | 1 | 1 | 0 | | |
| | Picket construction site | – | 0 | | | |
| | Settle for mid-size facility | 0 | 1 | | | |
| Elected Representatives | Support Citizens' Protest | – | 1 | | | |
| Government | Provide support to Project Group | 1 | 1 | 1 | | |
| Nature | Recession | | | 1 | | |
| | Disaster | | | | 1 | |
| | Technological development | 1 | | | | 0 |
| | Column number | 1 | 2 | 3 | 4 | 5 |

↑ Small facility now preferred by all as result of favorable technological development.

↑ Previous unilateral improvement for Project Group not preferred in recession ("sanction" by Nature)

↑ Reinforcement of credibility of sanction by Citizens' Protest as result of disaster

↑ Infeasibility due to lack of technology

* Coalition of Project Group and Government

100

The effects of natural and quasi-natural events can now be included in the analysis and can take their place in a strategic structure diagram relating to the problem in the form shown in Table 4.8.

In studying these effects, the question of the credibility of the interventions by Nature arises. A moment's reflection reveals that the credibility of Nature taking an option (as it might be assessed by a participant) is closely related to the subjective probability that he would assign to the event actually taking place. Methods of arriving at this subjective probability discussed in Chapter 3 can therefore be included in the analysis at this point.

## FACTORS THAT ARE TIME-DEPENDENT

In some complex decision problems, one or more of the options of the participants may be feasible only during certain periods of time. This can occur, for example, when the feasibility of the option depends upon the provisions of a contract or agreement of limited duration. It may occur, also, if an option is feasible only until a certain regulation comes into force. This might be the case when progressively more stringent regulations (regarding say, pollution) are implemented over a period of time. In other circumstances, an option may be time dependent in the sense that the cost of keeping open a choice between alternatives becomes unacceptable after a certain point in time. The effect on the analysis of options in all such situations is that the choice for or against implementing an option must be considered to be withdrawn for the participant concerned for the period of time that the option is not available (or introduced for the time that it is available).

In certain circumstances, the withdrawal or introduction of the option may be irreversible. This would be the case, for example, when the availability of an option is dependent on the existence of an agreement or contract that cannot be renegotiated. The lapsing of the contract would then cause the option to be irreversibly not available. As a special case, the alternatives represented by the options of Nature can often be considered to be irreversibly withdrawn when the event to which the option refers actually happens.

As an illustration of the manner in which options can be time-dependent consider the options in the "Construction of Facility X" dispute (Table 4.1) and the possible reasons why options might lapse or be introduced as shown in Table 4.9.

The availability status of an option in a given period can be taken

Table 4.9    Possible Time-Dependency of Options

| Participants | Options | Possible Reasons for Time-Dependency |
|---|---|---|
| Project Group | Continue construction of large facility | Excessive loss after a certain date if choice switched eventually to mid-size or small facility |
| | Build small facility at Site A | Technology available only after certain future date |
| | Settle for mid-size facility | Not desirable after certain level of investment in large facility |
| Citizens' Protest | Support Government in election | Option not to support Government has much less weight after imminent election |
| | Picket construction site | Not time-dependent |
| | Settle for mid-size facility | Time-dependency related only to possible future increase in desire for construction activity in area. |
| Elected Representatives | Support Citizens' Protest | Need to support may change after election |
| Government | Provide support to Project Group | Policies may change after election |
| Nature | Recession <br> Disaster <br> Technological development | Event may actually happen |

into account by use of a dynamic form of the analysis of options. The procedure consists initially of listing the time-dependency of the options and of forming tables of participants and options for each of the series of time periods in which the time-dependency causes a variation in this information. A convenient method of keeping track of which options are open to the participants at each of a series of future times is shown in Figure 4.4. In this diagram, the time-dependency of the options is that contained in Table 4.9. Future times at which analysis is to be conducted are indicated by vertical lines. The analysis is conducted in the normal fashion at each of these times using the appropriate listing of participants and options. The result is an evaluation of the strategic structure of the problem at each of these future times and an indication of any variation in the possible outcomes as time progresses. In particular, the results include a summary of the outcomes that become (a) possible or impossible and (b) irreversibly possible or impossible over the time period covered in the analysis.

This information may be of considerable importance in planning and in deciding the tactics that are to be used in any forthcoming negotiations with the other participants. Suppose for example, that the preferences of two participants for three possible stable outcomes A, B, and C are as follows:

|  | *Participant 1* | *Participant 2* |
|---|---|---|
| First preference | A | C |
| Second preference | B | B |
| Third preference | C | A |

Suppose, further, that outcome A is estimated as becoming irreversibly unavailable if the decision is delayed beyond a certain date. This might cause Participant 1 to press for acceptance of outcome A before that date. It might equally well give Participant 2 reason to attempt to delay the decision beyond the date in the hope of achieving at least his second preferred outcome B.

Another elaboration of the method provides for the introduction or elimination of participants in the analysis and for the withdrawal and introduction of possible courses of action according to perceptions of future changes in the elements of the environment. Insomuch as any change is considered certain, it can be included in the analysis relevant to the time period as an irreversible change. If a degree of uncertainty exists, the change can be considered as an option of Nature and the analysis related to this particular change can be conducted as outlined in the previous section. One further step in the analysis is to consider possible variations of the preferences of the participants with the passage of time and to assess the effect that such variations may have on the existence of stable outcomes. As with all analysis of this sort, however, the value of the results depends upon the validity of the assumptions that are implicit in the input data.

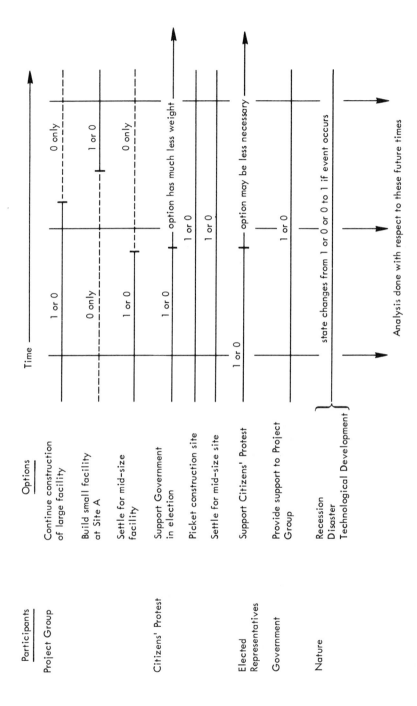

**Figure 4.4** *Method of Keeping Track of Availability of Time-Dependent Options*

## Testing the Results of an
## Analysis of Options

In most situations in which the analysis of options can be used, those conducting the analysis do not have complete information concerning the major factors involved. This lack of information does not refer only to the nature and likelihood of occurrence of future natural and quasi-natural events. The decision maker is also likely to have limited information available regarding: (a) the identity of all the participants in the problem situation; (b) the other participants' perceptions of the problem; (c) their objectivés and intentions; (d) their available options and alternatives; and (e) their preferences between scenarios. In addition, he may be in some doubt about the available options and preferences of the organization he represents due to lack of complete communication between the various levels and individuals concerned with the problem.

In such circumstances, it is natural that those with the responsibility for the decision should insert into the analysis their best estimates of all the parameters and values involved pending the collection of more complete information. However, much of the information contained in such estimates is likely to be subjective, depending (at least in part) on the perceptions, opinions, and experiences of those who formulate them. It is a wise precaution, therefore, to determine what effect changes in the estimates and assumptions used in the analysis would have upon the conclusions that have been reached. This can be done by a form of sensitivity testing that is analogous to the methods of sensitivity analysis used in the application of quantitative methods.

Sensitivity testing in this context consists of a deliberate program of variation of assumptions in the following categories: (a) the identity of the major participants and the options available to them; (b) the attitudes and preferences of the participants including those of the participant on whose behalf the analysis is being conducted; and (c) future possible natural and quasi-natural events and their probability of occurrence. The question asked in all cases is whether the conclusions of the analysis to date would be changed if the input assumptions were changed within a range considered possible but not necessarily likely. If little or no change in conclusions is detected over a broad range of assumptions, there is reason for confidence in the conclusions. If significant changes in conclusions result from the use of certain different assumptions, there is reason for caution in applying the analysis. Note that detection of possible changes in conclusions is no reason to reject the results of the analysis already conducted. Rather, it is more an indication that the conclusions may not have a sufficient quality of robustness to allow significant commitments to be made at this stage.

Sensitivity testing is important as a counter to unwitting misperceptions of the identity, options and the attitudes of the other participants in a decision situation.[13] There is evidence for example (as discussed in Chapter 3) that those involved in complex decision problems sometimes form stereotyped images of other participants despite ample information to the contrary. In the same way, options available to another participant are often ignored even when evidence of their existence is freely available. The effect of these misjudgements can be very great, perhaps because the very aspects that are often ignored are those that are most disadvantageous to the one who commits the error.

One way of guarding against the effects of misjudgement of other participants is to expand each participant considered in the analysis into a set of *pseudo-participants* based on the original characterization. In such an exercise, each pseudo-participant would differ from the original in a certain characteristic or attitude. For example, suppose that the attitudes and preferences assigned to Citizens' Protest and the Project Group in the analysis described earlier in this chapter are considered to be the most likely. The analysis can now be extended by investigating situations in which Citizens' Protest is characterized as *Aggressive* and *Timid* in comparison with the most likely attitude considered earlier and the Project Group as *Expansionary* and *Conservative*. Once these attitudes are reflected in the preferences for scenarios included in the analysis, a much wider range of possible circumstances is covered. This might reveal additional guaranteed improvements for certain participants with certain attitudes. A new light might be thrown on possible sanctions by virtue of the greater or lesser credibility of these measures that would be assessed as a result of the changed assumptions regarding attitudes of the participants.

Another form of sensitivity testing that results in a broadening of the field covered by the analysis concerns the options of the participants and the range of possible future events included as the options of Nature. In the example of the analysis given earlier in this chapter, terms such as small and mid-sized were used to describe the type of facility. In a practical analysis, however, these descriptions would be more specific and a wider range of characteristics would probably be included. This would allow a closer examination of the effect of facility size and characteristics on the conclusions of the analysis. In the same way, the option of Nature marked *Recession* might be replaced by a range of options distinguished by reference to a parameter such as a drop in gross national product. In addition, a range of probabilities of occurrence for each of these new options might be generated, rather than using a single value of this probability.

The further work involved in sensitivity testing may be regarded by some as costly, time consuming, and unnecessary, especially when pressures of time seem to dictate that the range of situations considered should be narrowed rather than enlarged. Nevertheless, the benefit of sensitivity testing lies in the greater degree of confidence in the results of a problem analysis and in the greater degree of insurance against unexpected developments in the later stages of the decision process.

## DISTINCTIVE CHARACTERISTICS OF THE ANALYSIS OF OPTIONS METHOD

One of the most important characteristics of the analysis of options is that the methodology provides a participant with an invitation (and the opportunity) to consider the viewpoint of the others involved in the complex decision problem with which he is dealing. Furthermore, it provides the opportunity for a participant to review his own perceptions both separately and in conjunction with those attributed to the other participants. The use of analysis of options helps to establish a forum in which multiple advocacy can be encouraged and in which the dangers associated with suppression of opposing and minority views in the early discussion of a complex decision problem can be lessened.

The analysis of options approach is soundly based on recent developments in the theory of games and metagames. However, despite its theoretical basis, the procedure involved in the analysis is readily understood by those without this specialized knowledge. It can be applied with the minimum of guidance from highly trained analytical personnel. It is, in fact, a method of analysis that responsible managers and decision makers seem to adopt naturally, probably because it parallels in many aspects procedures that they arrive at intuitively as a result of experience. Use of the analysis of options allows those responsible for complex decisions to take an active part in the analysis phase of the process of resolution, rather than delegating major parts of the analysis to specialists who do not bear responsibility for the final decision.

In using the analysis of options, the role of the specialist is that of providing support to the process of resolution rather than that of taking responsibility for major parts of the analysis. Continuing participation by those responsible for the decision is both necessary and desirable. They often bring insights and opinions to bear that are difficult to express in explicit or quantitative form and that might not, in other circumstances, be passed on to those to whom conduct of a major analytical study has been delegated. The integral involvement of decision makers in an analysis often leads to the development and expression of these intuitive opinions. In this way, the actual preferences of the responsible decision makers are inserted into the analysis. These preferences are based on their perception of the problem and on their implicit understanding of the background of the problem under consideration.

Because it conforms closely to procedures developed intuitively by experienced decision makers, the analysis of options is readily incorporated into the existing work of an organization. The logical step-by-step procedure gives assurance to those who are dealing with situations without apparent structure. It also helps to ensure that major features of the problem are not overlooked.

The analysis of options is not, however, a panacea that overcomes all the difficulties of dealing with complex problems. Nor does it offer a simple method of arriving at uniquely optimal and rational solutions to such problems. When decision makers are led to expect a panacea, their initial acceptance often changes to disappointment and disillusionment after a short period of trial.

What the method does offer is the opportunity to study the structure of a complex problem and to review the possible interactions of courses of action that could be selected by the participants in the problem situation. The progressive nature of the analysis allows understanding of the problem to grow as the work proceeds. Opportunities for resolution of the situation emerge as more and more aspects of the problem are considered. The logical development of the analysis also allows the introduction of new and different points of view into the considerations. The final result of the analysis is the sort of review of the strategic content of the problem that is a necessary preliminary to effective action by one or more of the participants concerned.

## SUMMARY

In most complex decision problems, the interests of the participants are in some degree of conflict. Such problems cannot be resolved by unilateral action on the part of one or other of the participants. Only outcomes that are jointly acceptable to the participants are likely to provide a stable resolution to the problem. Conflict and cooperation are, therefore, intimately linked together and some degree of conflict may be an integrative force in social and business affairs.

The second phase of the process of resolution of a complex problem is concerned with an analysis of the interaction of the preferences of the participants for future scenarios. This analysis can be conducted using an approach based on recent developments in game and metagame theory. The analysis is centered on the search for combinations of the options of the participants that would result in an equilibrium. An equilibrium is defined as a situation from which it is not to the advantage of any of the participants to move, provided that the others do not. All situations involving conflict of interest have at least one equilibrium of one sort or another. An equilibrium position may be desired by participants in a complex decision problem who wish to achieve a degree of stability rather than to continue in a state of conflict and confrontation.

A practical procedure for analyzing the structure of complex decision problems based on game and metagame theory is called the *analysis of options*. In this procedure, the first step is to define the participants and their options. Combinations of these options (called scenarios) are then studied to determine whether or not they constitute situations that could be the basis for a stable agreement, contract, or treaty between the participants. The purpose of this analysis is not to establish what the participants should do, but rather to determine what each and all could do if they decided to adopt certain attitudes towards the conflict situation in which they are involved.

A recent extension of the original analysis of options method allows the inclusion of natural and quasi-natural phenomena that are often important factors in complex problems. This is done by addition of a participant called Nature who is assumed to have *options* representing possible future events. Nature is not treated as a full participant, but is brought into the analysis when the occurrence of natural or quasi-natural events could affect the conclusions concerning the other participants. Further extensions of the original method allow for treatment of changes in the participants, in their available options, and in their preferences for scenarios with the passage of time.

Sensitivity testing of the results of the analysis of options is recommended as a means of examining the effects of changes in assumptions—with regard to the participants, their options, and their preferences—on the results. This leads to a broadening of the scope of the analysis and a corresponding increase in the degree of confidence that can be placed in the results. It provides also a degree of insurance against unexpected developments at a later stage of the decision process.

The analysis of options has certain distinctive characteristics as a method for analyzing complex decision problems. While it is soundly based in theory, it is readily appreciated by those without specialist analytical knowledge. Those responsible for complex decisions can, therefore, take an active part in the analysis rather than delegating much of the work to a specialist group. This allows insights and opinions to be brought to bear that may be difficult to express in explicit or quantitative form. Use of the method often makes for the establishment of a forum in which divergent views can be expressed and examined. The danger of suppression of negative and contrary opinion is therefore lessened.

The method conforms closely to procedures already intuitively adopted by decision makers and is therefore readily incorporated into the day to day work of an organization. However, the analysis of options cannot be regarded as a panacea to overcome all difficulties in dealing with complex decision problems. Its major purpose is to provide a review of the strategic structure of a problem as a basis for decisions on actions to be taken by one or more of the participants.

### DISCUSSION TOPICS

1. Is there a significant difference between the *single-party, multiple-objective* decision making problem and the problem with many parties, each with a single objective? If not, why not? If so, what are the key factors in the difference? Can one type of problem convert into the other and, if so, under what circumstances?

2. Can you think of any complex problems that can be treated realistically as single-party problems in the modern world? Why is there not more than one participant in these problems?

3. What are the dangers inherent in attempting to treat a complex decision problem by multi-objective decision techniques rather than by consideration of the elements of conflict by game theoretic methods?

4. An equilibrium looks like a good solution to a conflict problem. Why is an equilibrium not a uniquely rational solution to a complex problem?

5. What are the similarities between measures that can be adopted by decision makers to avoid or minimize uncertainty and those

that provide some degree of insurance against the effects of conflict?

6. Under what circumstances can a metaequilibrium be the basis for a stable contract or agreement between parties in a conflict situation? Does the conclusion of such an agreement alter the situation and would any such alteration affect the agreement?

7. How would you go about introducing the analysis of options into the discussion of a conflict situation in which you are involved at work or in your community? Do you think it could be adopted naturally when explained in everyday language or are there likely to be difficulties in others understanding the technique?

8. Why is it necessary to go to such lengths to explain what is covered by the analysis of options? Isn't it what most decision makers do intuitively? What does the method provide that is not already present in organizational decision making?

9. Decision makers in complex situations usually have only limited information. What effect does this fact have on the application of the analysis of options?

10. Do you think it is valid to represent possible future natural events and the actions of unknown participants by the addition of options of a participant called Nature? Are there objections to this procedure that you can put forward?

11. What are the similarities and differences between the analysis of options and the Braybrooke and Lindblom strategy of decision? Are these methods mutually supporting?

12. Braybrooke and Lindblom recommend that the decision process be continuous and that during the process, both *means* and *ends* be adjusted according to circumstances. What effect should this concept have on the use of the analysis of options in practical situations?

## REFERENCES

1. Simmel, Georg. *Conflict and the Web of Group Affiliations.* The Free Press of Glencoe, 1955, pp. 13–20.
2. Richardson, L. F. *Arms and Insecurity.* London: Stevens & Sons, 1960, pp. 12–36.
3. Rapoport, Anatol. "Lewis F. Richardson's Mathematical Theory of War." *Journal of Conflict Resolution* 1 (1957): 249–99.
4. For an introduction to these models, see M. Nicholson, *Conflict Analysis.* London: English Universities Press, 1970, Chapter 4; or K. E.

Boulding, *Conflict and Defense*. New York: Harper Torchbooks, 1962, Chapter 3; or the classic work by J. von Neumann, and O. Morgenstern, *Theory of Games and Economic Behavior*, 3rd ed. Princeton, N.J.: Princeton University Press, 1953.

5. Howard, Nigel. *Paradoxes of Rationality*. Cambridge, Mass.: The MIT Press, 1971.
6. Radford, K. J. *Managerial Decision Making*. Reston, Va.: Reston Publishing Co., 1975, pp. 136–45.
7. Howard, Nigel, *Paradoxes*, op. cit., pp. 127–46.
8. Radford, K. J. *Managerial Decision Making*, op. cit., pp. 148–72.
9. Howard, Nigel. "The Arab-Israeli Conflict: A Metagame Analysis Done in 1970." *Peace Research Society Papers* 19, The Ann Arbor Conference, 1971.
10. Bain, H., N. Howard, and T. L. Saaty. "Using the Analysis of Options Technique to Analyze a Community Conflict." *Journal of Conflict Resolution* 15 (1971): 133–44.
11. Alexander, Joyce M. "An Operation Analysis of Conflict in Northern Ireland: an American Perspective." *Journal of Peace Research* 13 (July 1976).
12. Howard, Nigel. "The Analysis of Options in Business Problems," *INFOR, The Canadian Journal of Operational Research and Information Processing* 13, No. 1 (February 1975) 48–67.
13. Janis, I. L. *Victims of Group-Think*. Boston, Mass.: Houghton-Mifflin Company, 1972.

# 5

# Communication, Negotiation, and Bargaining Between Participants

## INTRODUCTION

Analysis of the strategic structure of a complex decision problem does not generally yield a unique solution that would be immediately acceptable to all of the participants. It usually indicates only a range of possible outcomes that could result from different choices of courses of action by the participants, acting individually or in coalitions. Each of these outcomes may be more or less desirable from the point of view of the various participants and coalitions. No participant (or coalition) can necessarily obtain the outcome that is most preferred by him. Those participants that wish to achieve a stable resolution of the problem must seek it in terms of an outcome that is jointly acceptable to all.

The question of which outcome actually comes about is usually determined in a third phase of the decision process during which communication, negotiation, and bargaining takes place between the participants. This interaction between the participants may be explicit and direct, as in cases where they meet in an open forum. On the other hand, it may be much less direct. In some cases it may be conducted through an agent who is not directly involved in the decision problem. The tactics that a participant employs during this phase may have a considerable effect in determining whether he achieves an outcome that is favorable to him. The greatest part of this chapter is devoted to a discussion of these tactics.

The initial part of this discussion will be conducted (as in the two previous chapters) from the point of view of a single participant. However, as the argument is developed, the tendency will be to attain towards an overall view of the situation. In the same way, the initial considerations of tactics will be (as before) in the context of a single time slice or frame of the action. In the later stages, the dynamic nature of the interaction will be considered more and more as a necessary introduction to a continuous model of the process of resolution discussed in the next chapter.

## METHODS OF COLLECTIVE CHOICE

Participants in the third phase of resolution of a complex decision problem are engaged in a process of choosing jointly a particular outcome from among those available, under conditions in which each participant may have different preferences for the various outcomes. This process is essentially that of *social choice* treated by Arrow in his classic work first published in 1951.[1]

In this work, Arrow sought a general rule by which choices between alternatives can be made collectively on behalf of a group under circumstances in which the preferences of members of the group for the various options are not necessarily the same. In seeking this general rule, he laid down five conditions that he thought it could reasonably be expected to satisfy. These five conditions can be summarized as follows:

1. the group decision rule should be applicable over a wide range of conditions;
2. if one option or outcome rises or remains constant in the preference orderings of each member of the group, it must rise or remain constant in the collective preference ordering of the group;
3. if the individual preferences for any subset of the available options are unchanged, the group ordering for that subset should be unchanged also;
4. for any two available options, the group ordering must not be independent of the individual orderings (the Condition of Citizen's Sovereignty);

5. the group ordering must not coincide with the ordering of any one individual without regard for the orderings of the other members of the group (the Condition of non-Dictatorship).

Arrow proved that no general rule for decision making on behalf of the group could meet all the above conditions simultaneously.[2] The practical implications of this result are that any rule for collective decision that meets the above conditions in one situation may not be satisfactory under different circumstances. In addition, Arrow's theorem shows that any rule for collective choice that is expected to be applicable over a wide range of conditions must either take no account of at least some of the individual preferences (in contravention of condition 4) or be imposed by one member of the group regardless of the preferences of the others (in contravention of condition 5). This is not to say that agreement on a satisfactory resolution is impossible among participants with differing preferences for a range of available outcomes. It indicates instead, that no general rule for resolution in such cases is likely to be available.

In practical circumstances, each problem requiring collective choice is normally resolved on its merits by means of some form of interaction between the participants. In some cases, the preference patterns of those involved are not actually identical, but they have sufficient similarity to allow many collective choices to be made without major difficulty. Participants who are engaged together in a number of decision situations sometimes find that differences in their preference patterns diminish as a result of their continuing interaction. If the preference patterns of those involved are similar, the difficulties of the Arrow conclusion have much less force, and the process of resolution approaches that of individual choice.

Situations in which the preference patterns of the participants are markedly different are those for which the process of resolution is most difficult. In such cases, Lieberman has noted that a number of behavioral factors may influence the outcome.[3] For example, in many situations in which a collective choice between outcomes is required this is often achieved by one participant with the necessary power and authority making a choice unilaterally and choosing it on the others. This is unlikely to occur in situations where the power is equally distributed between the participants. However, if the majority of power rests with one participant, a dispute that has been tolerated for a while in the interests of free discussion of the issues may be ended by that participant imposing a solution. This may not be unwelcome to the others involved, since an imposed solution may be preferred at that stage to what may appear to be a fruitless continuation of the argument. The exercise of power provides a way out of the impasse in such circumstances.

Examples of the imposition of a solution by a powerful participant have occurred in recent strikes in a number of countries in which the public service is involved. After a period of negotiation that has proved fruitless, it is often judged by the government that continuation of the dispute is not in the public interest. The government then uses its power to introduce legislation to end the strike and to impose a settlement reached by means of a method such as compulsory arbitration. The difficult problem of collective choice is then replaced by what it is hoped will be a more tractable procedure of choice by a single party not directly involved in the dispute. Similar procedures and reasons are often behind the establishment of a commission or judicial enquiry to investigate complex disputes that do not appear to be moving towards a settlement by other means.

In situations in which all participants prefer a settlement to an indefinite continuation of the dispute, the relative strength of the preferences of the participants for outcomes is often an important factor in the resolution of the problem. If one participant perceives, for example, that the others involved have a strong preference for a particular outcome while his own preferences do not vary much between all outcomes, it may be to his advantage to concede that outcome to the others. The advantage may be in the good will generated by such a move. It may, however, be in the more tangible form of a benefit or side-payment or it may possibly be in expectation of a similar favor in some future decision situation in which all the participants are involved.

Recognition of strengths of preferences is implicit also in situations where a strong negative opinion about an outcome is held by a participant. In some situations, one such negative opinion is allowed to outweigh all other positive preferences. The veto procedure of the United Nations Security Council was established presumably with such considerations in mind. The basis of the procedure is a desire by all participants to retain a forum for discussion and resolution of disputes and not to risk the withdrawal of one who is threatened with the adoption by the majority of an outcome that he strongly opposes.

The process of collective choice is most often one of adjustment between the participants. This process of adjustment ultimately determines the relative benefits attained by each in the resolution of the decision problem. Lindblom has maintained that the adjustment often takes place naturally and without apparent purpose.[4] In many cases, however, it is achieved during a direct or indirect process of negotiation and bargaining between the participants. There is often considerable advantage to be had by a participant who makes a judicious choice of tactics to be used in the negotiation and bargaining process. The manner in which this choice of tactics can be made will now be discussed in detail.

## THE SETTING FOR NEGOTIATION AND BARGAINING BETWEEN PARTICIPANTS

The setting for negotiation and bargaining between the participants in a complex decision problem has three major components.[5] The first of these is the set of possible outcomes. Each participant enters into the negotiation phase with his own estimate of the set of possible outcomes determined by intuitive thinking or by a more formal process such as the analysis of options. Whatever the process of formulation, however, the actual estimate of alternative outcomes is subjective and is derived from the information available to the participant regarding the elements of the decision situation and from his perceptions of the preferences and circumstances of the other participants. At the start of the negotiation phase, therefore, it is possible that the views of the various participants on the set of possible outcomes may differ due to the different information in their possession and their consequent different perceptions of the problem. In the same way, each participant's perception of the strategic structure of the problem situation may be different. The actual difference between these perceptions in a practical situation depends in major part upon the variation in the content of the information sets available to the participants.

The second component of the setting for communication and negotiation consists of the preference patterns of the participants at the start of the negotiation phase. These are made up of three major contributing factors. The first of these factors is concerned with estimates of the benefits and disadvantages that are perceived to be associated with each of the possible future outcomes. These estimates are dependent on (and are derived from) such elements of the situation as values, standards of behavior, and levels of expectation of those concerned. The second factor contributing to preference patterns is the estimated cost or benefit of not arriving at a resolution of the problem at the particular time, influenced, possibly, by feelings that "time is on our side" or, on the other hand, that "time is running against us." The third major factor influencing the preference patterns is concern for the reputation of the participant in the conduct of negotiations and for the effect of present actions on that reputation in future situations of the same kind.

Each participant carries into the negotiation phase a set of initial images of the perceptions of each of the other participants of the possible outcomes and of their preferences between them.[6] These initial images are the third component of the setting. They are built up over time by observing behavior of the others involved, by studying their writings or verbal declarations, and possibly by previous direct communication between participants. The initial images of any participant are neither complete nor certain. It is common knowledge that there may be advantage to be gained by a participant in concealing information of this nature from the others involved, at least in the early stages of negotiation.

## COMMUNICATION IN NEGOTIATION AND BARGAINING

The essential ingredient of the process of negotiation and bargaining is exchange of information between the participants. The content of the messages exchanged is usually designed to influence the recipient in some way and to change his perceptions of the problem, his view of the possible outcomes, and his preferences between them. The communication may be tacit and indirect, such as sometimes can be achieved by a participant going about other business, apparently unconcerned, in what is thought by others to be a time of crisis. It may, on the other hand, be direct and explicit, in the form of a letter from one participant to another or a public statement. In between these two extremes, there is an infinite variety of types of communication, each comprising a mix of the tacit and explicit forms.

The information communicated by any participant may be considered by him and by others to be true or false or a mixture of both. The extent to which information that is considered to be false is deliberately imparted to others is a measure of the degree to which the participant originating the message is engaged in bluffing.

The objective of communication of information in the negotiation and bargaining phase is usually to influence other participants towards accepting a position considered to be advantageous by the participant offering the information. The degree of success attained in such an attempt to influence other participants is dependent on the nature of the message imparted, the manner in which it is delivered, and the perception of the recipients of the message of its contents. In general terms, the greater the uncertainty of the participants regarding the elements of the problem situation and their perceptions of the others' alternatives and perceptions, the greater is the effectiveness of information imparted in the negotiation and bargaining phase. By the same token, the greater that uncertainty, the greater is the possible advantage likely to accrue to a participant from the conveying of judiciously selected information in this phase.

## MOVES IN NEGOTIATION AND BARGAINING

The essential ingredient of communication in negotiation and bargaining can be achieved by a variety of moves that are available to the participants. These moves can be considered initially in two broad categories: (a) *pure communication moves,* in which information is passed that is designed to alter the participants' perceptions of the problem and their preferences for alternatives and outcomes, and (b) *structural moves* that involve commitment to an actual alternative, a broadening or a narrowing of the options available to one or more of the participants.

Pure communication moves do not necessarily involve an immediate change in the alternatives available to any of the participants. However, since the passage of information may result in the increasing or lessening of the number of alternatives considered feasible by a participant, such a change may be considered their actual effect. On the other hand, structural moves almost always result in an immediate change in the available alternatives, since they usually involve some form of action or commitment to action. Nevertheless, structural moves have an intrinsic information content. The two categories, therefore, shade into one another in many practical situations. Both bring about a change in the strategic structure of the problem situation by virtue of a change in the options available to the participants, a change in their preferences for outcomes, or both.

Moves in negotiation and bargaining may be *coercive* or *accommodative.*[7] A coercive move is one that is designed to apply pressure on one or more of the other participants intended to bring their position closer to that of the initiator of the move under threat of punishment if they do not comply. An accommodative move is one in which the participant making the move changes his position to what he believes is closer to that of the others in the hope that this will bring about an atmosphere conducive to settlement. Accommodative moves are usually conditional, offering a change of position as long as there is reciprocal action by the others involved. They often have a significant coercive component as, for example, in cases where it is indicated that dire consequences may be expected if the expected reciprocal moves are not forthcoming. Accommodative moves may also be made in the hope and expectation of benefits at a later stage of the negotiations.

Well-known bargaining moves can be placed in one of the four categories defined by combinations of four types of moves: coercion, accommodation, pure communication, and structural. For example, an accommodative pure communication move might be an offer of an unconditional concession. In contrast, one of the most familiar coercive pure communication moves is the *threat*. The purpose of a threat is to communicate an increase in the probability that an indicated alternative will be chosen and, thereby, bring about a change in the other participants' perceptions of the threatener's preference pattern. A threat is usually escalatory insomuch as new values in terms of the threatener's prestige or bargaining reputation are brought into the arena. Note that a threat is sometimes posed in the form of a structural move, particularly in situations in which some additional advantage occurs from the accompanying action.

Another form of pure communication move is the *promise*. A promise is, in many ways, the opposite of a threat since it implies reward for compliance as opposed to punishment for noncompliance. A promise is different from a threat insomuch as it is necessary to carry out the action specified (and to incur the attendant cost) only if the desired effect on the opponent is attained. In contrast, the action involved in a threat (the threatened punishment) is necessary only if the gambit is unsuccessful. The purpose of a promise is, however, similar to that of a threat. It is to demonstrate a strong preference for an indicated alternative and to provide an incentive for others to choose that alternative also. The promise is, therefore, often more coercive than accommodative, although it is usually not escalatory to the same degree as a threat, probably because some reward is offered for compliance.

Structural moves may also be accommodative or coercive. An accommodative structural move might for example be the removal of pickets from a construction site in a situation similar to that of the "Construction of Facility X" treated in the previous chapter. Coercive structural moves can be described under four headings: *escalatory, committal, circumventing,* and *fait accompli*.[8] An *escalatory* move is one that increases the level of conflict between the participants, usually by increasing what is at stake in the dispute. Introduction of nonunion labor is an escalatory move in an industrial relations dispute, because it challenges the position of the union while at the same time increases the chances of violence and of a long strike.

A *committal* coercive structural move is one that commits the participant to a position or course of action. Once the commitment is communicated to the others involved, notification is given of the preferences of the committing participant. For example, the closing of a factory by management in the face of a strike or the start of construction of a facility about which there has been considerable dispute are communications of commitment to certain outcomes and of strong negative preferences for others.

A *circumventing* coercive structural move is one designed to reduce the effect of a committal move. The introduction of nonunion labor may be a move circumventing a strike called by a union against an employer. In the same way, the call for a boycott of the goods and services offered by the employer is a move circumventing the use of nonunion labor. Finally, the *fait accompli* is a coercive structural move in which a new option is introduced or an existing one eliminated in a surprise action. Such a move is often designed to increase the risk of an unsatisfactory outcome as perceived by other participants who may, as a result, take some counteraction in answer to the fait accompli. It is usually undertaken as a direct challenge to the previously communicated positions of other participants when, for example, a lockout is instituted in answer to the threat of a strike.

In practical negotiating and bargaining, tactics usually consist of a mix of coercive and accommodative moves of both the pure communications and structural types. Coercive moves often appear to offer more advantage in the early stages of negotiations, when it may be desirable to stake out positions as a preliminary to a later concession. The danger in placing too much emphasis on coercive moves at any stage in negotiation or bargaining is that such tactics may lead to escalation of the conflict and make it more difficult to achieve an atmosphere of trust. On the other hand, there is usually little advantage to be had from making a unilateral concession at the start of negotiations. An early and firm statement of position by one participant often sets the stage for negotiation towards that position, to the ultimate advantage of the participant making the original statement. The art of negotiating and bargaining is in the choice of appropriate tactics in situations in which the perceptions of the various participants may not be identical.

## COMMITMENT, CREDIBILITY, AND RISK
### IN A CONFRONTATION

Negotiation and bargaining are processes in which each participant is guided by his perceptions of what the others involved in the decision situation will ultimately accept. In situations in which all the participants have different most-preferred outcomes, resolution requires that all or some of them accept an outcome that is less satisfactory than had been desired. This concession is made since, at some point in the bargaining process, the loss in accepting an outcome that was originally less preferred is considered by the participant conceding to be less than the expected loss associated with continuing the dispute. It has been argued (particularly by those taking a game theoretic approach to negotiation and bargaining[9]) that if a participant can demonstrate an irrevocable commitment to a particular outcome and can convince the others of his determination not to revoke that commitment, that participant is most likely to succeed. The best initial bargaining tactic by any participant in such a situation is said by adherents to this line of thought to be to express openly a unalterable determination to bring about the outcome most preferred by him.

There are, however, some difficulties in carrying out this tactic in practice. Its success depends not only on the participant actually incurring an appropriate commitment, but also on his communicating to all the others involved his absolute determination not to back away from that commitment at some future time. The degree to which he achieves this communication determines the credibility of the commitment in the eyes of the other participants. In assessing this commitment, the others involved normally take into account the behavior of the participant advertizing the commitment in earlier situations of the same type, his standing within his organization or community, and his apparent mandate for negotiation of the particular issue under consideration. Other factors that affect the credibility of a commitment are its reversibility, assessed in terms of the ease with which it can be cancelled, and the cost associated with such a reversal. For example, a structural move involving expenditure of a great amount of money and effort is likely to be afforded considerable credibility. A simple statement of intent is normally given less credence, unless there are other factors, such as the commitment of the reputation of the person involved, that add to its credibility.

Each participant in the decision situation does not have exactly the same impression of the degree of credibility of another's commitment. The varying impressions are due to the subjectivity of the interpretation by the participants of the information content of the moves that are made to demonstrate the commitment. They are also due to the different stored impressions of the previous behavior of the participant expressing the commitment.

In addition to this subjective estimate of credibility, each participant can be assumed to have an intuitive feeling regarding the degree of risk of a less satisfactory outcome that both he and his opponents might incur in a continuation of the confrontation. Each participant in the negotiations and bargaining has also a perception of the maximum risk that his opponents can tolerate at any point of time.[10, 11]

The choice of tactics by any participant in negotiating and bargaining can be envisaged as deriving from the interaction between his perceptions of the commitment of all concerned to their stated positions and his assessment of the level of risk felt by each of them with respect to a continuation of the confrontation. If a participant assesses the risk of continuing the confrontation (in the light of his perceptions of the credibility of the others' commitments) to be acceptable for the time being, he may be expected to remain firm in his determination to obtain his most preferred outcome. On the other hand, if the estimated risk is higher than he can tolerate, he might be expected to explore the possibilities of settlement. Furthermore, a participant may be expected to lean towards more coercive tactics in dealings with a participant whose tolerance for risk is assessed as being low and to be more conciliatory if his acceptance of risk is regarded as high.

As an example of the interaction of perceptions of credibility, commitment, and risk, let us consider the situation near the end of World War II. In a much simplified view of the situation, it can be assumed that, after the German surrender, there were three possible outcomes available to the major participants, the Allied Nations (a coalition of which the U.S. was a major partner) and Japan. These possible outcomes can be described briefly as follows:

1. *U.S. Victory*, comprising Japanese surrender and most preferred by the Allied Nations;

2. *Japanese Victory*, naturally most preferred by the Japanese;

3. *Negotiated Peace*, after a considerable prolongation of the war, the second most preferred outcome of both participants.

Although the situation was obviously much more complex than is indicated by this brief description, it is likely that these outcomes appeared prominently in the explicit or intuitive assessments of the strategic structure of the problem by both sides. The conduct of the war can be thought of simplistically as a series of moves in a negotiation and bargaining phase of the dispute (the continuation of diplomacy by other means) in which the objective of both major participants was to bring about the outcome most preferred by them. Many of the moves were of the structural type involving invasions, occupation of territory, and creation and dismantling of alliances. Some were pure communication moves concerned with propaganda and attempts to influence opponents by passing information that was often of dubious quality to the other side.

In the period between the early Japanese successes and the first half of 1945, changes in the strategic structure of the dispute were not great. After the German defeat, there was some apparent quickening in these changes although it was clear to both sides that ending the war by conventional means and achieving their most preferred outcome would be a slow and costly process. However, it appears from reading history that neither side considered the risk of continuing the war to be beyond their tolerance at that time.

The situation was changed abruptly by the successful testing of the atomic bomb, although only one side knew initially of the imminent availability of this terrible weapon. The question of how it should be introduced into the bargaining and negotiation activities represented by the continuing conduct of the war must have been considered very carefully in the Allied councils. Note that the introduction of this weapon did not change the overall strategic structure of the problem. The possible outcomes remained broadly the same. The possibilities of one or other of the participants bringing about each of the possible outcomes were, however, significantly altered.

The primary objective of introducing the weapon was not to kill hundreds of thousands of people (although this tragically occurred) but to raise the level of risk to the Japanese of continuing the war beyond a level tolerable to them. The problem facing the Allied war councils was essentially how the existence of the new weapon could be made known to the Japanese in a manner that would make its effect on the war situation (and the Allied commitment to use the weapon) most credible and would, therefore, drive the Japanese estimates of risk beyond the tolerable level. Two broad categories of moves were available: structural and pure communication.

The recorded history of how the choice of move was made is sketchy, but it seems that at least three possible alternatives were considered, namely: (a) a pure communication move of openly describing the bomb and its likely effects; (b) a pure communication move of inviting observers to a demonstration at an uninhabited site; and (c) a structural move with significant communications content involving an actual attack. How the conclusion was reached to make the third type of move need not concern us at this point, although it is certain that a prime consideration was the delivery of an unequivocal and, therefore, entirely credible message. As the situation turned out, the credibility of the threat was established after some initial confusion, and the desired effect of raising the perceived risk to the Japanese of continuing the dispute was achieved.

Not all negotiation and bargaining situations are as clear-cut as the preceding description might imply. It is possible for example that two or more participants might consider the credibility of the others' threats and determination to maintain a commitment as being so low that neither would feel that his risk in continuing the dispute was intolerable. In these circumstances, continuation of the dispute is likely and escalation of the stakes may occur, much in the same way as in a game of poker. Once escalation is attempted by one or another of the participants, new estimates of credibility and risk are made by all and these determine the later conduct of negotiations. On the other hand, it is possible that at some stage in the negotiation and bargaining phase all participants perceive that the credibility of the others' threats and determination to maintain a position is such that the risk to them is greater than their various tolerable levels. In such cases, all participants will seek a settlement and this will be facilitated by a series of accommodative moves in the later stages of negotiation and bargaining.

## COERCIVE TACTICS IN NEGOTIATION AND BARGAINING

Coercive tactics in negotiation and bargaining are tactics aimed at modifying the perceptions of the other participants in such a way that the credibility of one's own position is increased or the apparent risk to them of not coming to a settlement is raised, or both of these occur. These tactics consist of the use of one or more coercive moves designed to produce some or all of the following effects:[12]

1. to reduce one's apparent net cost of continuing the dispute or of possibly escalating it;
2. to increase one's apparent valuation of what is at stake thereby increasing the apparent cost of backing down and the apparent value of winning;
3. to increase one's apparent determination to stand firm and thereby to increase the credibility of one's position;
4. to increase the opponents' estimates of the net cost of continuing the dispute and of any possible escalation of it;
5. to reduce the opponents' estimates of the value of winning the dispute and thereby to decrease the perceived cost to them of coming to a settlement.

The manner in which these effects might be achieved is described in the following paragraphs.

*Reduction in one's apparent net cost of prolongation or escalation of the dispute.* This can be brought about by structural moves that have the effect of increasing the alternatives available and the capabilities of the participant to cope with the effects of the dispute. This could involve a switch of orders from a struck manufacturing plant or the selection of an alternate source for goods or services denied by an opponent. Structural moves of this sort have an inherent communications content. This can be enhanced by pure communications moves in which the beneficial effects of the introduction of the alternatives are stressed and possibly magnified and in which the deleterious effects of the actions of the other participants are minimized.

*Increasing one's apparent valuation of the stakes.* There are a number of pure communication moves that can have the effect of persuading opponents that one's valuation of the stakes (and therefore the cost of backing down) has been increased. These include:

- making statements to the effect that one's prestige, honor, and future bargaining reputation have become involved in the dispute or alternatively, making threats that, unless a settlement is reached quickly, these considerations will unavoidably become involved;
- coupling the settlement of the current issue with a larger confrontation with very high stakes. This can be achieved by pointing out that the current dispute is in reality only part of a much wider problem situation in which all the participants are involved. The implication can be made that one's resolution, actions, and achievements in the "smaller" dispute (and more particularly how these are assessed by the other participants) will have significant effects on one's bargaining power in other related disputes and ultimately on the outcome of the "larger" situation.
- citing and legality, traditional correctness, moral rectitude, and fairness of one's position and indicating that any movement away from that position would constitute a major breach of firmly held principles;
- invoking obligations to those who depend on success in the current negotiations and responsibility to see that these obligations are met.

*Increasing one's apparent determination to stand firm.* A number of coercive tactics are aimed at increasing the other participants' estimates of one's determination to hold to a stated position and thereby increasing the credibility of that position in the eyes of the opponents. The most powerful of these is the structural move of undertaking an irrevocable commitment that eliminates the possibility of retreat or concession. A less powerful version of the same gambit is the pure communication move of threatening to become irrevocably committed unless a quick settlement (on one's own terms) is achieved. This real or threatened burning of bridges allows a participant to maintain during bargaining that he is in no position to compromise. Furthermore, it has the effect of transferring to the opponents the initiative and the burden of proposing a move towards a settlement that must of necessity be accommodative and, therefore, likely to result in an outcome less satisfactory to them.

A similar effect can sometimes be achieved by protestations to the effect that one is unable to make concessions because these would immediately be repudiated by the interests that a participant represents. This tactic is often employed by national leaders in negotiations with other countries who say that public opinion at home would not countenance such a concession. The credibility of such a move can often be reinforced by messages received from the negotiator's constituency during the course of bargaining that reaffirm determination not to move from the established position.

Commitment to a particular position can be reinforced by delegating responsibility in the negotiation and bargaining to an agent who has demonstrably less flexibility and who has been given instructions in a manner that is visible to the other participants forbidding any concession or change from the established position.

Much the same effect can be achieved by a participant making himself unavailable for the receipt of communications of any sort. In doing so, the participant who is out of touch lets it be known that he cannot be deterred from his commitment by receipt of news of others' commitments. However, the appropriate circumventing move may be to feign ignorance of the opponent's inability to receive messages, thereby hoping to deter his commitment by virtue of an unwitting commitment on one's own part.[13]

There are many pure communications moves that may increase the credibility of one's determination to stand firm. These range from constant expressions of confidence to suggestions that one's own position is the only defensible one and that a "rational" opponent will eventually come to see the situation in this way. A related gambit that serves to increase one's apparent commitment to a position is to represent it as being the result of certain natural forces over which man has little or no control and of which one has unique and detailed knowledge.

*Increasing an opponent's estimate of the cost of continuing the dispute.* Many of the tactics designed to decrease one's own apparent cost of prolongation of a dispute can also be used to increase an opponent's estimate of the cost of continuing the confrontation. These tactics consist of structural moves that have the effect of increasing one's available options and associated pure communication moves in which one's cost of not settling are minimized and invulnerability to the opponent's moves are stressed. Moves of both kinds that provide evidence of support from others, whether they are participants in the decision problem or not, are also often effective in increasing the opponent's net costs of not conceding.

It may also be possible to stress the danger that continuation of the dispute will lead to escalation and the greater attendant risks of such developments. These risks can be magnified also by the use of a threat that leaves something to chance. The normal type of threat is a statement of what one *will* do if the opponent does not comply with certain conditions that are specified. The power of this tactic depends upon the credibility of the commitment to the punitive action or, in other words, the degree of certainty of punishment for not complying. The disadvantage of the tactic is that the opponent may discount the effects of the punishment in advance and that the resulting non-compliance requires that the punitive action (which may be costly to both sides) be taken in order to protect the credibility or bargaining reputation of the threatener.[14]

In making use of a threat with a random ingredient, it is made known that, although there is every intention to carry out the punitive actions if there is no compliance, the actual decision as to whether the punitive actions are implemented is not altogether under the threatener's control. The scale of the possible punishment in the original threat can therefore be increased, because the actual implementation of the punitive actions can be stopped if necessary at some later stage by invoking a real or imagined intervention by another party or event.

*Reducing the opponent's value of winning.* In the same way that engaging prestige, honor, and bargaining reputation can be used to increase one's apparent valuation of what is at stake in a dispute, moves intended to decouple these factors from a settlement can serve to reduce an opponent's perception of his actual risk. This can be done by providing a path towards settlement (or a rationale for settlement) that permits the opponent to comply with the minimum loss of face. It can be stressed that an opponent's behavior in the particular dispute at hand will in no way be considered to be indicative of his general attitudes or of his possible behavior in future confrontations. The present situation can be represented as special and unlikely to occur again and future issues to be totally different in character, so that the opponent could be expected to act differently on future occasions.[15]

Another technique is to represent the present issue as one of little importance to the opponent, so that little will be lost in conceding in this instance. The implication is that different behavior would be expected in dealing with future issues of greater relative importance. Then again, the present issue can be said to be of such great importance to oneself that apparent success must be obtained at all costs. However, the impression can be given that this is the last such issue that is likely to occur and that one will be much more reasonable on future occasions. This technique has been used successfully by many world leaders and depends on the fact that most of the concern for the effect of present actions on future bargaining capability depends on the assumption that one is facing a persistently aggressive opponent in a series of confrontations similar to the present situation.

Another method of reducing an opponent's valuation of the stakes involved in a dispute is to maintain that the confrontation has arisen naturally and not by virtue of aggressive behavior on anyone's part.[16] The opponent can then be called upon to resolve a mutually unsatisfactory state of affairs. In such circumstances, he may feel that his own prestige is not involved if a concession is made. He may even be persuaded that his prestige will be enhanced by taking a "statesman-like" initiative towards a settlement. A similar tactic that may result in a reduction of an opponent's estimate of his actual risk is to stress the service that he would do for the larger community in not prolonging the dispute. In all such cases, it is desirable to praise the opponent after he has conceded for his statesmanlike and farseeing approach to the problem.

An extension of the above tactics is to claim that the situation under dispute is, in some way, abnormal or not legitimate. This tends to devalue what is at stake in the mind of an opponent, particularly if a seemingly unbiased third party can be represented as questioning the normalcy or legitimacy of the situation.

## Circumventing Tactics

Circumventing tactics are those designed to reduce the effect of coercive tactics and in many cases consist of opposite moves designed to counter the effect of those of an opponent. For example, a possible defense against an attempt by an opponent to couple his prestige and honor into what is at stake in a bargaining situation is simply to make moves designed to uncouple these factors. In other circumstances, demonstrating the legal basis for one's position is often an effective counter to attempts to represent it as illegal and abnormal. Stressing the perceived importance of the present outcome in consideration of future issues is a method of resisting the isolation of a dispute and a consequent devaluation of what is at stake.

## SOME DISADVANTAGES OF
## COERCIVE TACTICS

*To force To*
*To Something*

Although coercive tactics are an essential part of the approach of a successful bargainer and negotiator, their use, unmindful of the effects on both the threatened and the threatener, can lead to an unprofitable prolongation of the dispute rather than to its quick resolution. For this reason, the choice of any coercive tactics to be used in a given situation is a matter of very great importance to which considerable attention should be given before any particular move is implemented.

Some coercive moves may have much less effect on an opponent than is originally estimated. It may be, for example, that the costs that might accrue from noncompliance after a threat has been made had already been taken into account by the opponent in arriving at his decision not to concede. The threatener is then left with the unsavory and probably unrewarding task of inflicting a cost on his opponent that has already been totally or partially discounted. The tendency in such cases is to increase the threat in order to maintain face. This often leads to escalation that may be involuntary and unwanted. The actual costs of noncompliance may of course be greater than had been estimated by the opponent, but in most cases it seems to be the other way round. People adapt readily to circumstance and what may have been awe-inspiring when its dimensions were unknown often turns out to be less fearsome in the actual experience.

Implementation of threatened actions against an opponent often has other disadvantages. The greater the cost inflicted on an opponent, the greater the investment he may feel he has in his position and the less the chance that he may feel able to concede. Furthermore, each cost imposed on an opponent lessens the range of punishment that is still available to be threatened and, therefore, restricts future choices of coercive tactics.

One of the most seductive and potentially dangerous aspects of a threat is that it appears to offer immediate advantages without the necessity of an immediate payment of the costs.[17] Furthermore, since the nature of a threat is that its fulfillment is not necessary if it succeeds, there seems to be a chance that no cost at all will be incurred by use of the tactic. However, if the threat does not succeed, the postponed bills may be larger than had been taken into account at the time that it was issued. These postponed costs may be in terms of bargaining reputation and credibility if the threatened action is not taken or they may be in the form of actual amounts expended if the threat is carried out. Further costs may be incurred in such circumstances in the form of accusations from others of brutality or amorality in carrying out the threatened actions.

Another dangerous aspect of coercive tactics is in the effect that they may have upon the behavior of the participants in a negotiation.[18] The use of threats as a method of informing other participants may well be better than a complete absence of communication between those involved. However, a situation in which the only communication is by threats and warnings is likely to be unstable and dangerous for the following reasons:

- the participants' freedom of choice is limited by the commitments that are embodied in the threats. Whereas this is a desirable feature of the tactic in dealing with a less determined opponent (for example, in situations analogous to the game of Chicken) it increases the chance of prolongation of the conflict (and possible mutual disaster) against a more resolute participant;

- issuing a threat puts a participant's reputation and credibility at stake so that he is often committed to punish noncompliance even at high mutual cost. Not to do so may be interpreted as a sign of weakness and as an invitation to counterthreats;

- a threat may be issued requiring an opponent to do something that he had every intention of doing anyway. The threatener may then obtain a false perception from his apparent success and may be tempted to escalate his threats;

· a threat may be inappropriate because the perceptions of the participants of the situation are (unknown to each other) significantly different. A threat that is intended to be defensive in nature may be seen to be aggressive and provocative by the opponent in such circumstances. In order to be effective a threat must be specific and must be issued in a manner that leaves very little room for doubt. If the threatener does not appreciate the degree of uncertainty surrounding his perception of the circumstances and that of his opponent, there is a high probability that a specific threat will be misunderstood;

· aggressive threats may induce resistance in an opponent rather than compliance, increasing the attendant risk of escalation. They may create fear and hatred that have the effects of creating solidarity in an otherwise divided group and of triggering escalatory counterthreats;

· threats may increase the level of stress experienced by an opponent and thus cause him to be less flexible in his future conduct of the negotiations.


### THE NEED FOR ACCOMMODATIVE TACTICS


The preceding considerations of the decrease in flexibility and the increased possibility of escalation coupled with uncertainties regarding the behavior of an opponent under stress raise the question of whether it is wise to employ coercive tactics throughout prolonged negotiations. Many participants enter into negotiations with coercive tactics uppermost in their minds on the grounds that the first to make such a move may gain some initial advantage. As the bargaining and negotiations proceed, however, and as the risks of a prolonged and mutually unprofitable dispute become apparent to the participants, there often arises an awareness of a common interest in arriving at a jointly acceptable resolution of the problem. The manner in which such a resolution can be brought about may not be immediately apparent to the participants, particularly if an escalation of threats and warnings has led to sharply reduced flexibility and an increase of stress. Nevertheless, participants are often led in such situations to modify their coercive efforts and to investigate alternative tactics that may have more accommodative effects.

The introduction of accommodative moves into negotiations and bargaining involves a shift of emphasis from the conflicting interests of the participants towards those interests that they may have in common. The problem for each participant is to realize the common interest in a settlement while, at the same time, minimizing losses to his own particular self-interests.

Accommodative moves usually involve a concession. The greater the concession, the greater may be the chance that the opponent will accept and that this will lead to a resolution of the problem. On the other hand, the greater the concession, the greater is the likely loss to the self-interest of the participant conceding. The participant engaged in accommodative moves therefore seeks a balance between three factors: (a) the chance that the opponents will accept, (b) the loss to self-interest if the concession is accepted, and (c) the loss to self-interest if the concession is *not* accepted. This latter factor involves two other considerations: (i) the degree of difficulty that would be experienced in moving back to the previous position once the concession had been rejected, and (ii) the chance that the opponents will interpret the concession as a sign of weakness and stand firm on their positions in the hope of receiving further concessions.

The aim of the participant offering the concession is to persuade his opponents that he will stand even firmer on his new position having made what he represents as his maximum possible concession. The difficulty perceived by all participants considering a concession is that a shift towards accommodative tactics may be perceived by an opponent as a sign of weakness or lessening of resolution and may therefore be taken by him as a reason to increase the level of his coercive tactics.

The interaction between participants engaged in accommodative moves is, in many ways, similar to that in which coercive moves are concerned. The credibility of an opponent in both cases refers to the strength of his resolution to continue the dispute on the basis of the positions that he has outlined. In the case of an accommodative move, if it is judged that this is a small concession that if not accepted will be followed by a larger step, the credibility of the opponent is low and the estimated risk of continuing the dispute for a while is likely to be correspondingly low. However, if it is thought that the concession is truly the last an opponent can and will make, the credibility is high and the risk of continuing the dispute may exceed a participant's tolerable level. In such circumstances, the concession may lead to a settlement, possibly on the basis of a reciprocal act that establishes good faith in the negotiations.

## ASSURANCE

Participants in negotiation and bargaining are faced with the problem of selecting a judicious balance between coercive and accommodative tactics. The danger of a miscalculation of this balance resulting in overemphasis on coercive tactics is that the dispute will escalate. The danger from an overemphasis on accommodative tactics is that other participants may perceive this as a sign of weakness and endeavor to press for an advantage. The originator of the concession may then resort to coercive tactics on the grounds that concessions have failed to bring about a settlement and escalation may occur.

An essential consideration in the choice of tactics is that the conflict not be allowed to escalate through a threshold beyond which it becomes self-fuelling and destructive of the means of resolving and containing it.[19] The location of this threshold is determined primarily by the nature of the relationships between the participants and the constraints and assurances that they feel by virtue of their common associations. These constraints and assurances may or may not result in the containment of the conflict over a particular issue. The result of any particular confrontation does, however, affect the relationships between the participants and may have a significant effect on the resolution of later problems in which some or all of the participants are involved. This effect on the constraints and assurances implicit in the membership of the participants in a unit of society may be the most important result of a confrontation.

Although coercive moves are effective in limited aspects of negotiation and bargaining, they are often destructive of the constraints and assurances of membership in the common cause of resolving a conflict. One method of approach to this dilemma consists of adopting tactics that deliberately combine coercion with what is called *assurance*.[20] Such tactics are designed to maintain the element of challenge inherent in the different preferences of the participants for outcomes, but to do so in a manner that minimizes the possibility that the challenge will be considered to be intimidating by the opponents. Assurance is conveyed by indications that, whereas the challenger intends to pursue his own interests as far as this is possible, he also is committed to a relatively benign form of conflict and to an eventual settlement as long as his opponent is prepared to act in a similar manner. Assurance can be provided by an explicit or tacitly agreed set of arrangements or rules by which the scope, escalation, and threat levels of the conflict can be limited.[21] These arrangements might include methods of ensuring that channels of communication are kept open, checking the authenticity of messages exchanged through these communication channels, and agreeing in advance on individuals who might be mutually acceptable as intermediaries at various stages of the future negotiations. Nor do these arrangements need to be agreed between opponents prior to the negotiations. Unilateral prior signalling might serve just as well, as long as steps are taken to ensure that the message can be remembered by the opponent at some later time and referred to by him as a prior condition to the negotiations.

Assurance can be given to an opponent during negotiation and bargaining by combining an accommodative with a coercive move or by the deliberate and well publicized choice of a coercive move that is less threatening than others that are available at the time. Selection of blockade by the U.S. rather than air strikes during the Cuban crisis is an example of such assurance. The element of challenge is not diminished by such tactics. The purpose is to test the will of the opponent for paths that will lead to mutual benefit rather than escalation while, at the same time, not relaxing determination to act in one's own interests.

The advantages of negotiation and bargaining tactics based on a mixture of threat and assurance accrue to all participants in a dispute. They include a reduction in the chance that the situation will move out of the control of the participants as a result of escalation due to miscalculation. As compared with tactics that are purely coercive, those containing some degree of assurance provide the opportunity for striking a balance between threats and accommodation. They provide also an atmosphere in which all participants can respond to proposed changes while, at the same time, safeguarding their interests. Adoption of assurance tactics also creates a tendency for the coercive measures chosen to be less extreme and for threatened actions to be more in line with what is actually possible in the circumstances surrounding the dispute. The emphasis shifts from the inflicting of loss on an opponent to the choice of outcomes from which there will be mutual gain.

Paradoxically, the use of assurance as a tactic is likely to be more difficult when an opponent is weak, embittered, or paranoid. Under such circumstances, any challenge may be construed as an attack. On the other hand, if the weakness arises from internal dissension, the use of assurance rather than threats may have the effect of strengthening those of moderate opinion within the opponent's camp and allowing a reciprocal response to be generated.

## SOME GUIDELINES FOR THE CONDUCT OF
## NEGOTIATIONS AND BARGAINING

The essence of negotiation and bargaining is in applying the correct blend of coercion, accommodation, and assurance at any time during the interaction. Because there are many factors involved and because exact measurement of these factors is usually impossible, bargaining and negotiating are likely to remain an art rather than being subjected to formalization and specification in the manner in which many other less complex processes are treated. Nevertheless, some attempt can be made to state general principles upon which the conduct of bargaining and negotiation can be based and to formulate some guidelines for the selection of appropriate tactics in practical situations. The objective of the following paragraphs is to formulate some such principles and guidelines, based on practical experience and the work of those already referred to earlier in this chapter.

### An Important Preliminary

An important preliminary step before engaging in any move in negotiation and bargaining is to review the strategic structure of the decision problem. This review should be based on the latest available information concerning the elements of the problem that are judged most likely to affect the range of possible outcomes. In many practical situations the most important of these elements are: (a) the participants and their relative power to influence the final choice of outcome; (b) the alternatives or options available to these participants; (c) their estimated preferences between possible outcomes; and (d) possible future natural and quasi-natural events and their chance of occurrence.

Care must be taken to avoid bias and misperception at this stage, particularly with respect to the characteristics of the other participants, their intentions, their options, and their preferences. Factors that can lead to such misperceptions include distortion of the image of an opponent as a crafty and cunning enemy and the exaggeration of a self-image stressing virility and the morality of one's actions.[22] Positive measures to reduce misperceptions include the search for characteristics in an opponent that are attractive in human terms and the kindling of empathy with other participants in the problem under consideration.

Misperceptions are often reinforced by the unconscious rejection of information that is contrary to presently-held views and by the rejection of minority opinions as in the group-think phenomenon discussed in Chapter 3. Misperceptions can lead to a distortion of the perceived strategic structure of a decision problem and to errors in the selection of bargaining moves. Furthermore, in cases where one or more participant has such misperceptions, the interpretation of moves by the participants is likely to be markedly different from that intended. The consequence in such cases is often that all moves are considered to be scheming and coercive and the risk of miscalculation and escalation is high.

One partial safeguard against such misunderstandings is to devote a portion of the available time before starting any negotiating and bargaining session to a study of the decision problem as it probably appears to the opponents. This study can be supported by information gathered in the earlier phases and by current impressions as the negotiation unfolds. The study should include consideration of the sensitivity of the strategic structure of the problem (as it is perceived at the time) to changes in the assumptions made in the analysis of options. If time and available resources allow, a separate team might be set up to represent the principal opponents, to simulate how they may be regarding the present situation, and to predict the bargaining moves that might appeal to them.[23] This type of activity prior to bargaining frequently provides protection against surprise moves by an opponent and allows those engaged in the negotiations to appear to be well briefed and confident. In situations in which a great deal is at stake, it may be desirable to formalize this simulation activity into a series of gaming sessions that consist essentially of a rehearsal and practice of many possible directions in which the forthcoming negotiations might lead.[24]

### Clarity or Ambiguity in a Bargaining Move

The question of how clearly or how ambiguously the communication intended in a bargaining move should be expressed is of major importance and may have a significant bearing on its effectiveness. Fisher has proposed that such communications should be formulated in what he calls a *yesable* proposition, a message "with such clarity that it is in the form to which the single word 'yes' would be an effective answer."[25] He cites as a major advantage of such clarity the fact that formulation of messages of that sort requires considerable preparation. A yesable proposition is, therefore, likely to be well thought out whereas one in a more ambiguous form may be less clear primarily because the thinking behind it is more vague and the background considerations less well prepared.

There are arguments in favor of and against both clarity and ambiguity.[26] For example, maximum clarity in threats often results in maximum credibility and the threatener is seen to be firmly committed to a position or a line of action. In many circumstances, an explicit and unambiguous message is more likely to move the negotiations toward a settlement because of this firm commitment and because of the correspondingly high cost of retraction to the participant initiating the communication. Furthermore, a clear and explicit message is likely to penetrate "noise" caused by other more ambiguous communications and clear up misperceptions of some or all of the participants. It is likely also to present a specific set of alternatives that can be analyzed by all and that can be the focus of future negotiations.

On the other hand, a more ambiguous offer can be more easily disavowed if this seems to be necessary at some later time. This freedom of action is usually obtained only at some cost in credibility as the ambiguity may be interpreted as a sign of weakness by an opponent. However, an ambiguous threat may be less provocative than a clear and explicit demand. Furthermore, the freedom that an ambiguous threat provides in choice of future moves may be a considerable advantage, particularly in the early stages of negotiation when information on an opponent and his reactions may be scarce.

Clarity in accommodative moves usually enhances the chance of a settlement, but often acts against the self-interest of the participant initiating the message. In contrast, clarity in coercive moves usually works in favor of their success, but may be against the interests of all participants in that the chance of escalation is also increased. Clarity is, of course, not synonomous with rigidity. It is possible, for example, to be specific in a message that describes a number of possible alternative courses of action in detail. Rigidity would enter the message only if it contained a specific commitment to one of the alternatives under all circumstances.

### Formulation of a Bargaining Move

The impact of a bargaining move is often as dependent upon the manner in which it is framed and presented as it is upon the actual content of the action or communication. Consideration of how a threat, offer, or proposal may appear to an opponent lessens the risk of misperception on his part of the intention behind the move and may also lessen the chance of escalation of the confrontation as a result of misunderstanding. Such consideration involves studying the value systems, norms of behavior, and principles of the opponents as well as a review of their behavior in past bargaining sessions of a similar nature.

It is possible also to formulate a bargaining move in such a way as to make it more palatable to an opponent without lessening the degree of coercion or accommodation (or the mixture of both) that it contains. This can be done by offering rewards in terms of what is important to the opponent (rather than to oneself) and by including additional items that are of little import to oneself but that are highly valued by the opponent. It is of no consequence in the negotiations that these additional items are of little value to the participant offering them. The important factor is the opponent's subjective perception of the rewards offered for compliance, because it is this perception that determines the degree of influence exerted by the offer. The effectiveness of a threat can be increased in a similar fashion by framing the punishment for noncompliance in terms of those items that are most important to the opponent.

Many of the same effects can be obtained by phrasing a communication in such a way that the state of affairs that it seeks to bring about appears to be legitimate and a natural consequence of the present situation. This can be done by formulating demands or offers in such a way that they appear to be consistent with actions taken by an opponent similarly affected in the past. The citing of a precedent may make it easier for the opponent to conform because he can represent to the world that he is merely acting in a manner consistent with custom and past experience. A demand that seeks the reestablishment of conditions that existed in the past may be easier for an opponent to agree to than a totally new situation, irrespective of the relative merits to him of the two positions.

Another method of establishing the legitimacy of a demand or an offer is to point out that its provisions affect all participants in the same way. This is unlikely to be exactly correct but if the position that it is desired to establish appears to affect both sides equally, it may be easier for an opponent to accede to the demand. In the same way, a demand that appears to be consistent with previously established law or practice usually has a greater probability of success than one that refers to new and untried conditions and positions. Legitimacy can be established also by phrasing the communication in such a way that it appears to reflect the view of a well-known and supposedly impartial third party.

It is particularly important that coercive moves be formulated in the most legitimate manner possible. This involves relating the demands and the consequences of noncompliance as directly as possible to the decision that the opponent is being required to make. The effectiveness of the threatened consequences is also likely to be greater the more directly they refer to the individuals involved in making the opponent's decision. As Fisher points out "a threat to let the air out of the tires of an illegally parked car is more legitimate than a threat to inflict unrelated harm such as breaking a window in the house of the owner."[27] Furthermore, the effectiveness of a threat is likely to be greatest and the consequences most legitimate when the demand and the threatened action are closely correlated with the time when the opponent affected must make the decision whether or not to comply. A threat of action next month if the opponent does not comply today is likely to be much less effective than one in which there are immediate consequences of noncompliance.

### Decomposition of the Problem and the Moves

In many negotiating and bargaining situations, it is best to approach the resolution of the problem by a series of steps rather than to tackle the whole task at one time. This process of decomposition of the problem and of the issues involved has been called "fractionating" by Fisher.[28] It has the merit that progress can be made in some directions while other negotiations are stalled. The piecemeal approach to resolution also allows participants to make concessions on issues that are of minor importance to them without prejudice to their interest in other more vital matters.

The moves involved in negotiations and bargaining can be decomposed also. This is particularly effective when the act to be deterred or encouraged can also be broken down into a series of steps which have a cumulative effect. In such cases, a threat that is geared to the increments may be more effective and less dangerous to both parties than one that must be implemented (or not) when some stated critical level has been reached. A similar effect is obtained with a threat in which the severity of the punishment increases with the passage of time such as in a siege in ancient times or in the surrounding of a gunman in a modern urban setting. Tactics of the same sort are available to the participant who is threatened. If the acts necessary to his compliance can be divided into steps, he may be able to stave off the threatened punishment for some time by performing some of the initial steps, while hoping for a change of circumstances (possibly due to a natural or quasi-natural event) with the passage of time.

It is often advantageous to formulate promises and agreements in terms of a number of small, successive steps, particularly in circumstances in which no participant is willing to trust the others to implement an agreement involving the whole issue. However, if mutual trust can be built up on a series of small matters, each participant has the opportunity to demonstrate his interest in coming to an agreement with a minimum of loss if the others eventually prove untrustworthy. Even if the main issue cannot be divided in this manner, it may be possible to create the same atmosphere of trust by preparatory negotiation and agreement on a separate matter of minor concern to the participants.

### Breaking an Impasse

There are a number of ways of breaking an impasse that has arisen in a negotiation. A deadlock of this nature usually occurs when the participants are at the conflict point and no means seems to be available to bring about communication leading to the choice of a jointly acceptable outcome. Methods of breaking the deadlock are primarily aimed at initiating communication and contact between the participants. They can be summarized as follows.

A participant can restate his position in the hope that his opponents' subjective perceptions of that position will change. The restatement may be designed to include a small concession that it could be argued was already implicit in the original phrasing. Even if no such concession is included, the restatement itself may allow an opponent who had previously been required by his constituency to remain adamant to claim that a concession had been made and that a reciprocal action would be in order. Furthermore, a restatement may allow an opponent to make a favorable decision without the embarrassment of apparently reversing a previous stand. Much the same effect can be obtained by seeming to change the issue at stake by describing it in different words or by splitting it into component parts to be dealt with one at a time. Whether it is a position or an issue that is restated, something may be gained by making an offer more specific so that less speculation is possible about the real intent. Tactics of this sort allow negotiations to start anew, without prejudice to previous positions, because something seemingly new has been placed on the agenda.

In situations in which more than one opponent is concerned, it may be possible to restate the issues and possible methods of resolution in such a way that less pressure is placed on one opponent and more on another. This may result in an opponent who feels relieved by the restatement joining in the call for resumption of negotiations on the basis of the "new" conditions. It may possibly be followed by the creation of an implicit or explicit coalition between former principle opponents with the objective of reaching a settlement at the expense of a third participant.

A review of commitments within coalitions is appropriate if an impasse has been reached. It may well be that a coalition that was constructed at an earlier time has served its purpose and that it could be replaced to the advantage of one, if not all, of its members. A restructuring of coalitions immediately raises new opportunities for settlement either because the strategic structure of the decision problem is changed, because the preference structures of the new coalitions are different than those previously existing, or because the power structure between the coalitions has been changed.

A participant can create an initiative in an impasse by replacing his chief representative in the negotiations. Even if the stated position of the participant is unchanged, the change of personnel raises the possibility of a different approach in bargaining and the engaging of a different set of values in the negotiations. Furthermore an actual change in position can be signalled by selecting a suitable new representative. For example, if it is desired to signal a desire for a settlement, this can be done by selecting a new representative who is known to be a hard-liner and instructing him to make a public statement slightly less bellicose than would be assumed to be normal for him.

The wide range of tactics under this heading includes a call for a mediator that immediately requires each of the participants to explain his position. The work of a mediator is, in essence, to transmit interpretations of these positions between the participants and to receive signals from them that otherwise might not be made for fear of the consequences of unilateral concessions.

## SUMMARY

The analysis of options in a complex decision problem serves to determine the strategic structure of the problem and to indicate a number of possible outcomes. Which of these outcomes actually comes to pass is determined by negotiation and bargaining between the participants, who are, in effect, engaged in a process of collective choice among alternatives.

The theorem of Arrow states that no general rule for collective choice can be formulated as long as the preferences of the individual participants for the various outcomes are substantially different. However, this does not prevent such choices being made in individual cases, although the exact nature of the process of choice may vary from situation to situation. In practical circumstances, the exercise of power by one of the participants is often a major factor in the choice. More generally, the strengths of the preferences of the various participants often influences the choice of outcome and these are brought to bear during the negotiation and bargaining phase of the decision process.

The setting for this phase has three components: (a) the set of possible outcomes, (b) the preference patterns of the participants over these outcomes, and (c) the initial images of the participants about the others' perceptions of possible outcomes and their preferences between them. Negotiation and bargaining consists essentially of communication between the participants with the objective of changing their perceptions of these three components. The aim of any one participant is usually to influence others to accept a position more favorable to him.

The means employed in negotiations and bargaining consist of a variety of moves that may be described as (a) pure communication moves, (b) structural moves, and (c) a mixture of both. Both pure communication and structural moves impart information. However, structural moves result in an immediate change in the alternatives available to the participants, while pure communication moves may not. A move may be coercive or accommodative. Coercive moves often appear to offer more advantage in the early stages of bargaining, while accommodative moves are more common when a mutual interest in settlement has built up in a prolonged dispute. The most familiar coercive move is the threat. A promise is often more coercive than accommodative.

There is often considerable advantage to be had in bargaining in expressing a firm commitment to a particular outcome. In order to do this, however, a participant must first incur an appropriate commitment and second make his commitment credible to his opponents. Once the commitment has been expressed, other participants make their own assessments of the risk to them of continuing the dispute in the light of this information. A useful model of the bargaining process takes into account the degree of risk of an unfavorable outcome that a participant can tolerate. If the perceived risk exceeds the tolerable level, a participant is likely to seek a settlement: if not, he is likely to prolong the dispute in the hope that others' levels of tolerable risk will be exceeded. The interaction of the credibility and of the tolerable risk levels of the participants then determines the outcome that is chosen.

Tactics in bargaining can be considered in terms of the degree to which they enhance the credibility of a participant's commitment to a given outcome or increase the risk to an opponent in continuing the dispute, or both. However, continued use of coercive tactics designed to increase credibility and an opponent's risk can result in escalation of the dispute. It may also result in stress on the opponent that sharpens individual behavior patterns. The risk of miscalculation and misperception is also increased. At some time during the negotiations and bargaining, therefore, participants often modify their coercive moves and investigate alternative tactics that may have considerable accommodative elements. The risk in so doing is that such a shift may be interpreted as evidence of weakness of commitment.

Participants in negotiation and bargaining are faced with the problem of selecting tactics that have a balance between coercive and accommodative elements. One method of approach to that problem is in terms of tactics that combine challenge with indications that the conflict will be kept within limits. However, this approach is likely to be less effective against opponents who see themselves as weak. On the other hand, if the weakness is due to internal dissension, such tactics may strengthen the hand of moderates in the opponent's camp.

Although choice of tactics must be made for each situation individually, some guidelines can be formulated for the conduct of negotiations and bargaining. For example, an important preliminary step is to check available information and subjective perceptions of the elements of the situation. Sensitivity testing of analysis of the strategic structure should be undertaken. Choice of the degree of ambiguity or clarity to be included in communications should be considered carefully. The impact of a bargaining move is often as much dependent on the manner in which it is framed and presented as on the actual content. It may be possible to decompose the issues or the moves so as to achieve more progress towards a settlement by steps rather than by an assault on a larger problem. It is possible, also, to break an impasse in a manner that does not signal weakness or loss of resolution.

### DISCUSSION TOPICS

1. How is bargaining affected by the fact that each participant's appreciation of the strategic structure of the decision problem is likely to be different?

2. How does the relative power of the participants affect the process of collective choice of an outcome? If one participant is relatively much more powerful, does he necessarily dictate the outcome?
3. Why is communication of information the essence of moves in bargaining and negotiation?
4. Can you think of examples of structural moves in a bargaining situation that had little information content? Were any such moves proposed in, say, the Cuban Missile Crisis? Would they have been effective in your opinion?
5. Do you agree that coercive moves are usually more advantageous at the start of bargaining and negotiation? Are there basic reasons behind your conclusion?
6. Is a promise the opposite of a threat? If so, can promises be coercive? Are promises less desirable moves because compliance requires payment of the promised reward?
7. Does the credibility/risk concept assist you in visualizing the interaction in bargaining? If so, what are its disadvantages? If not, can you propose a better model?
8. What is the relationship between the credibility of a move and its reversibility? Is any move completely reversible?
9. How can a move that increases the alternatives open to a participant affect the balance in a bargaining situation? In what situations would you employ such a move?
10. What are the advantages of coupling the settlement of the current issue with other issues with very high stakes? Are there advantages also in some situations of decoupling issues? Can you give examples?
11. How may the introduction of an agent acting on behalf of a participant affect the conduct and outcome of negotiations?
12. Under what conditions might it be advantageous to use a threat with a random ingredient? Are there any attendant dangers in using this tactic?
13. Stress encountered in bargaining may sharpen individual behavior patterns. How could this affect the outcome of negotiations? Does the possibility of an opponent coming under stress make certain tactics less desirable?
14. When are accommodative moves desirable in bargaining? How can these moves be initiated without loss to self-interest?
15. Can the credibility/risk concept be applied in the case of accommodative moves? What are the differences between its application to coercive and accommodative moves?
16. Can you give examples of the use of assurance in bargaining situations? In particular, can you think of situations in which assurance

was given unilaterally without disadvantage to the participant taking this initiative?

17. Can you propose general guidelines for determining the degree of clarity or ambiguity desirable in a message in a bargaining situation?

18. What methods can be used of making bargaining moves more palatable to an opponent without lessening the impact of the coercion or accommodation intended?

19. How can the apparent legitimacy of an offer or of a demand be enhanced?

20. What are the advantages of decomposition of an issue or of a bargaining move? Are there any potential disadvantages of this technique?

21. What are the uses to which formation or dissolution of coalitions can be put during bargaining?

22. What are the useful roles of a mediator in negotiations? Can proposing a mediator be an advantageous tactic and, if so, under what conditions?

## REFERENCES

1. Arrow, K. J. *Social Choice and Individual Values.* New Haven, Conn.: Yale University Press, paperback edition, 1973. (Originally published by John Wiley & Sons as Cowles Foundation Monograph No. 12, 1951.)
2. Ibid., p. 59.
3. Lieberman, Bernhardt. "The Study of Collective Decisions." In *Decision Making*, edited by H. S. Brinkers. Columbus, Ohio: Ohio State University Press, 1972, pp. 42–66.
4. Lindblom, C. E. *The Intelligence of Democracy.* New York: The Free Press, 1965, p. 3.
5. Snyder, G. H. "Crisis Bargaining." In *International Crises: Insights from Behavioral Research*, edited by C. F. Herman. New York: The Free Press, 1972.
6. Kriesberg, Louis. *The Sociology of Social Conflicts.* Englewood Cliffs, N.J.: Prentice-Hall, Inc., 1973, pp. 28–34.
7. Snyder, G. H. "Crisis Bargaining," op. cit., p. 222.
8. Ibid., p. 223.
9. Schelling, T. C. *The Strategy of Conflict.* New York: Oxford University Press, paperback edition, 1963, pp. 24–28.
10. Zeuthen, Frederick. *Problems of Monopoly and Economic Warfare.* London: Routledge and Kegan Paul, Ltd., 1930, Chapter 4.

11. Walton, R. E., and R. B. McKersie. *A Behavioral Theory of Labor Negotiations*. New York: McGraw-Hill, 1965, Chapter 3.
12. Snyder, G. H. "Crisis Bargaining," op. cit., pp. 229–231.
13. Schelling, T. C. *The Strategy of Conflict*, op. cit., p. 26.
14. Ibid., pp. 187–203.
15. Snyder, G. H. "Crisis Bargaining," op. cit., p. 234.
16. Richardson, J. L. *Germany and the Atlantic Alliance*. Cambridge, Mass.: Harvard University Press, 1966, pp. 252–54.
17. Fisher, Roger. *International Conflict for Beginners*. New York: Harper & Row, 1970, p. 40.
18. Lieberman, James E. "Threat and Assurance in the Conduct of Conflict." In *International Conflict and Behavioral Science*, edited by Roger Fisher, Basic Books, 1964, pp. 110–22.
19. Vickers, Geoffrey. "The Management of Conflict." *Futures*, Vol. 4, pp. 126–141.
20. Lieberman, James E. "Threat and Assurance," op. cit., pp. 119–22.
21. Schelling, T. C. *Strategy of Conflict*, op. cit., pp. 77–80.
22. White, Ralph K. *Nobody Wanted War*. New York: Doubleday, 1968, p. 6.
23. Shlaim, Avi. "Failures in National Intelligence Estimates: the Case of the Yom Kippur War." *World Politics* 28 (April 1976): 373.
24. Shubik, Martin. *Games for Society, Business and War*. Elsevier Scientific Publishing Company, 1975, pp. 203–243.
25. Fisher, Roger. *International Conflict*, op. cit., p. 15.
26. Snyder, G. H. "Crisis Bargaining," op. cit., pp. 247–48, and 252.
27. Fisher, Roger. *International Conflict*, op. cit., p. 149.
28. Fisher, Roger. "Fractionating Conflict." In *International Conflict and Behavioral Science*, edited by Roger Fisher. New York: Basic Books, 1964, pp. 91–109.

# 6

# Models of the Decision Process

The discussion to this point has been concerned with the component phases of the decision process and with the details of methods and techniques that can provide some degree of guidance to a participant in a complex decision problem. The starting point of the exposition was a description of the characteristics of complex decision problems and the manner in which they differ from those that can be resolved using formal analytical methods. The elements of a complex problem were then described and the discussion led from there to a detailed treatment of the three phases that are involved in the resolution of such problems, consisting of:

1. a first phase in which a participant: (a) reviews the information relevant to the problem in his possession; (b) sets about gathering such additional information as he considers is necessary and feasible to obtain; (c) formulates a perception of the problem; (d) specifies courses of action that he believes he and others might implement to bring about what they may consider to be a more desirable future; and (e) generates estimates of his own and others' preferences for possible future scenarios.

2. a second phase in which each participant evaluates (intuitively or by formal analysis) the strategic structure of the problem,

148

determines which outcomes he considers might be stable, and assesses his preferences between outcomes;

3. a third phase in which information is exchanged between participants regarding their perceptions and preferences and from which agreement on a jointly acceptable outcome may emerge.

These three phases can be considered as the components of a first simple model of the decision process, as illustrated in Figure 6.1.

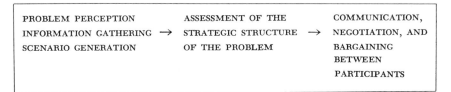

Figure 6.1   *A Simple Model Showing Three Phases of the Resolution of a Decision Problem*

However, this simple model is not adequate to represent the manner in which complex decision problems are resolved in practice. It does not, for example, illustrate the important features of interaction and iteration between the activities in each of the phases. Nor does it include any representation of the continuing nature of the process of resolution that results from the constant search for information and the continual reassessment of the problem and possible methods of resolution.

## Decision Making as a Continuing Process

The continuing nature of the manner in which complex decision problems are resolved can be clearly seen when one observes the work of those dealing with such problems in practice. The method of approach to most of these problems consists of a continual evaluation of available information, followed by a choice of measures judged necessary at the time. Even decisions of a fundamental nature, which constitute only a small proportion of all those encountered, are usually preceded and followed by a sequence of incremental steps.[1]

Strategies that have been recommended to decision makers for dealing with complex problems put stress on the continuing nature of consideration of these problems. For example, the strategy of

*fractionating* (a means for avoiding a confrontation between participants by dealing first with minor aspects of a larger problem) involves a process of resolution of a problem in which continuous and
successive approaches are employed rather than a single concerted
attack.[2] In similar fashion, the emphasis in incrementalism is on the
continuing review of the problem, of the objectives and ends that it
is desired to achieve and of the effectiveness of measures selected
for implementation as the process of dealing with the problem unfolds.[3] The strategy of incrementalism is, in fact, closely linked to
the concept of "piecemeal social engineering" in which progress is
made by a continuous series of small steps towards a more desirable
future situation.[4]

Similar emphasis is found in the prescription for decision making
called *mixed scanning*. It is recommended to those adopting this
strategy that the implementation of a course of action and the commitment of resources to the implementation be divided into a sequence of steps. A procedure for review of the results of the earlier
steps is included in the strategy. Plans for subsequent steps can be
adjusted in the light of this review and of any additional information
that is gathered as the implementation proceeds. It is recommended
further, that the more costly and less reversible steps be positioned
to the greatest extent possible in the later stages of the planned implementation so that the greatest degree of flexibility is retained for as
long as possible.

These recommendations are consistent with concepts of planning
in which a plan is seen as a set of interrelated and sequential decisions prepared to guide an individual, organization or community
over some future period of time. Since the environment surrounding
the plan is changing continuously, a plan prepared in this manner
needs to be updated, extended, and adjusted as time unfolds. Actual
experience can then be compared with expectations expressed in the
plan, the cause of any deviations identified, and any corrective action
found to be required can be incorporated in a new version of the
plan. This method of proceeding lessens the effect of future contin-
gencies on the activities of those who are working to the plan and
provides for the continual assimilation of new information as it becomes available.

A plan prepared in this manner and consisting of a timed sequence
of decision points is essentially an instrument designed to control to a
significant degree the future activities of all those involved in a decision problem. Because of the increased rate at which the environment
of complex problems is changing, organization procedures designed to
implement such plans and to control future activities must be capable

of rapid and frequent changes that may often be of significant dimensions and scope.[5] In order that this can be accomplished effectively, a capacity for adaptation and learning must be an essential part of the design of such procedures. The ·scope of the adaptive and learning capability required must range over revisions of objectives, ideals, and expectations; considerations of value systems and norms of behavior; and reassessments of the characteristics, preferences, and attitudes of all other participants in the complex problems under review.

## FORMULATION OF A MODEL OF THE CONTINUING DECISION PROCESS

Provision for the continuing nature of the process of resolution of complex decision problems requires modification of the simple model shown in Figure 6.1. A first step towards envisaging a more comprehensive representation of the process is shown in Figure 6.2. In this diagram, time is depicted as unfolding from top to bottom and the three phases of the process of resolution are spaced across the page. Information gathering, analysis, and assessment leading to perceptions of the problem and to the formulation of courses of action is shown as a continuous bar to the left of the diagram. It is depicted in this manner to emphasize the continual impact of new and processed information on the perceptions of those involved in the decision process.

The central part of the decision process is shown under the heading "strategic evaluation" as a series of frames that represent periods of concentrated consideration of the problem. In actual organizational activities, these frames might be sessions of a task force charged with consideration of the problem, portions of regular management meetings devoted to the particular problem, or just periods of time during which a single decision maker devotes his attention to the problem. The frames are shown dotted at the top and bottom of the diagram to give the impression of a continual process of consideration, the part shown in full lines being only a part of the process selected from the whole for the purposes of illustration.

Arrows from the information gathering and analysis bar to the frames denote that there is a regular flow of new information and perceptions into the strategic evaluation. Distances between successive frames are shown as variable to emphasize that these considerations need not (and in most cases, should not) be at fixed intervals. The process of adaptation and learning requires that reaction to new information and circumstances should be flexible. The period of time

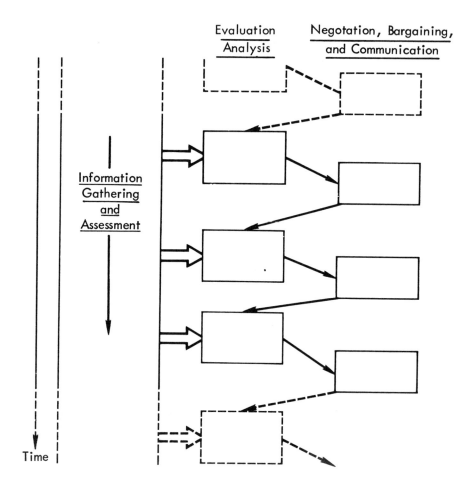

Figure 6.2  *Diagrammatic Representation of Treatment of a Complex Decision Problem by One Participant*

between sessions of strategic evaluation depends, therefore, on the nature of the decision problem at the time and on the perceived urgency of taking some action. In more urgent circumstances, the frames might be expected to move closer together and in less urgent cases to move further apart in time.

The agenda that is followed in any one of the strategic evaluation frames is similar to that illustrated in Figure 6.3.

1. Review of position at end of last session
2. Introduction of new information and perceptions
3. Reassessment of the strategic structure of the problem
4. Selection of actions necessary at this time

**Figure 6.3   *Typical Agenda of a Strategic Evaluation Session***

The first item on this agenda is a review of the position reached at the end of the previous session. This item is comparable to the reading of minutes in a conventional committee meeting. This is followed in the second item by a review of new information and perceptions, derived from formal information gathering and assessment activities (represented by the bar to the left of Figure 6.2) and from other less formal activities such as personal contacts and meetings. The results of communications with other participants and perceptions of their reactions to actions taken to date by each of those involved in the decision problem are an important input into this item on the agenda.

Once this new information has been introduced into consideration, a reassessment of the strategic structure of the problem can be undertaken. This is followed by the selection of any immediate actions that are considered necessary at this particular stage of the decision process. These actions might be substantive in the form of a structural move designed to enhance the position of the participant in the continuing decision problem. Such actions might involve commitment of large amounts of resources. On the other hand, the actions might be in the form of pure communication moves designed to influence the other participants toward accepting a particular outcome.

There are several important considerations in the selection of actions to be implemented at this stage. The first is the reversibility of the move. If the desire is to be seen to be committed to a course of action, a move that is costly to reverse once implementation has been started may be necessary. If, on the other hand, the requirement is to influence the other participants without incurring costly commitments, a more easily reversible pure communication move, delivered with much apparent firmness, may be more desirable.

A second important consideration in selecting actions to be taken at this time is the time-dependency of the factors that constitute the decision situation. If it is estimated that none of these factors is likely to change in the foreseeable future, the choice of action can be made purely on the basis of moves considered desirable in the forthcoming negotiation and bargaining phase. On the other hand, if certain of the factors involved were judged to be time-dependent, it will have been necessary to include this aspect in the reassessment of the strategic structure. The choice of actions can then be made with knowledge of the effects of the time-dependency on the availability of possible outcomes. Actions that are necessary to bring about future scenarios that may not be available at some later time may then be of prime importance. Alternatively, a decision can possibly be made to delay action in anticipation of more favorable circumstances that will arise at a later date.

Other considerations at this stage concern the amount of information regarding the selected actions that is to be imparted to each of the other participants and the manner in which the communication is to take place. For example, some or all of the other participants may be kept in the dark beforehand in order to present them with a *fait accompli*. Alternatively, one or more of the participants may be informed before the action is implemented as a means of providing assurance. Communication of the information might take place at a single meeting of the participants. On the other hand, it might be part of a more continuous process of information release and reception over a period of time. Both forms of communication are represented by the boxes to the right of the diagram. Each participant notes the information received in the negotiation and bargaining phase and returns it as input to his next strategic evaluation session. The cycle is then repeated for as long as the particular decision being considered is of concern to the participant.

The model of the decision process in Figure 6.2 is crude and needs to be refined for application to any particular case according to the characteristics and circumstances that surround it. Nevertheless, the model shown is sufficiently a representation of the various aspects of the decision process that have been discussed to this point in the text to allow it to be used as a starting point for further elaboration and refinement.

### Introduction of Many Participants into the Model

The model in Figure 6.2 relates to a single participant only. A first step in elaboration of this model is to include a representation of other participants in the decision problem. This is done in Figure 6.4. Certain details included in Figure 6.2 have been omitted in this new diagram for the sake of clarity. However, they can be transferred mentally to the new diagram as is found necessary for detailed consideration.

In Figure 6.4, the strategic evaluation sessions of the various participants are shown by a vertical series of frames in each case. The input of information and perceptions from the participants' individual information gathering and analysis activities is indicated by the arrowhead to the left of each frame. Note that the information and perceptions that are entered into the strategic evaluations are not necessarily the same for each participant. Nor are the strategic evaluation sessions of the individual participants necessarily coincident in time.

From time to time, participants communicate with one another concerning their perceptions of the problem and with regard to any actions or moves that they have decided to take as a result of their strategic evaluations. This exchange of information is represented in Figure 6.4 by boxes labelled "communication." Not all the participants are necessarily involved in any one exchange of information. A participant may decide to communicate certain information to only some of the participants that are known to him. Others may be deliberately excluded or their participation in the problem may be unknown to the initiator of the communication. In cases in which the information is imparted more widely, such as by a public statement, this may not be noticed by one or more of the participants, or it may be ignored.

### Linkages between Problems

A further elaboration of the model is shown in Figure 6.5, which illustrates linkages between coexisting decision problems. In this diagram, the single decision problem considered to this point is shown centrally, flanked on either side by problems that are "horizontally" linked. These are problems that exist at essentially the same level in the organization or community, that may have participants and other elements in common, and that may be such that actions taken in respect of one problem have some effect on the others. Also shown in the diagrammatic representation of Figure 6.5 are two problems that are linked to the original one in the vertical or hierarchical sense. Note that no attempt is made in this diagram to represent the action space of the problems (which might be disjoint or overlapping)

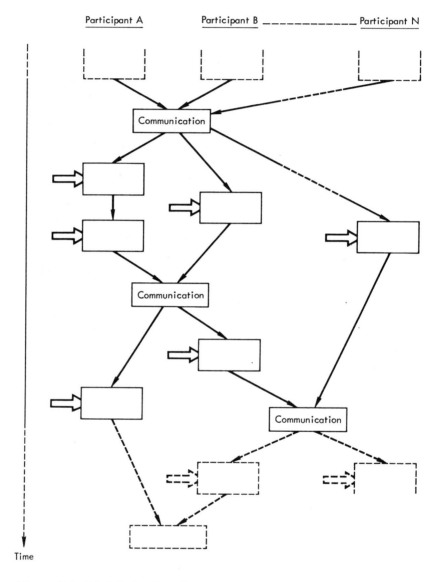

Figure 6.4   *Model of a Complex Decision Problem with More Than One Participant*

156

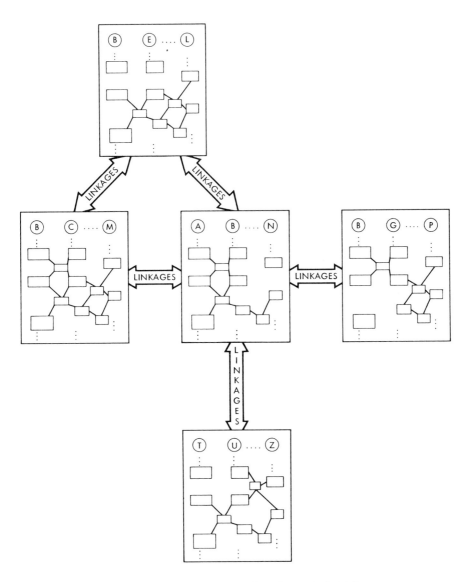

Figure 6.5 *Diagram Showing Horizontal and Vertical Linkages Between Problems*

or the relative time sequence in which the resolution process unfolds in each of the problems.

One important type of hierarchically linked problem concerns relationships between the various interests that may exist within a participant. Suppose, for example, that participant A in the problem shown centrally in Figure 6.5 is an organization that consists of a number of groups with different interests that meet from time to time to decide the position that should be taken on behalf of the organization as a whole in the central problem. The process of defining that position may itself be a complex problem in which the various groups within the organization are the participants. This hierarchically subordinate problem is linked to the broader one and might be represented as the lower central panel in Figure 6.5.

The attitudes, preferences, feasible courses of action, and negotiation moves of participant A in the central problem are then dependent to a greater or lesser extent on the activities in the internal problem in which the component groups are engaged. If there is unanimity among the component groups concerning the whole or a part of the issue in the larger problem, the statements and actions of the representatives of the organization in that problem are likely to be credible. On the other hand, if the component groups are clearly at odds, the position of the organization's representatives in the larger problem is likely to be much weaker. Examples of this effect can be found in many practical complex problems. The credibility and negotiating capability of union representatives in an industrial relations dispute depends upon the solidarity of the membership. The position of a U.S. President or Secretary of State in negotiations with another country depends upon the state of affairs in the internal, linked problem in which elements of the executive and legislative branches of the government are involved in determining foreign policy and the methods of implementing it.

## THE RELATIONSHIP BETWEEN THE MODEL AND ACTUAL EXPERIENCE

It is always desirable when proposing a model of a process to consider whether it describes in acceptable fashion past experience in practical encounters with the process under examination. In the case of complex decision problems this is difficult because: (a) it is only recently that the resolution of complex decision problems has been subjected to concentrated study, and (b) there are only a few examples of detailed documentation of complex decision problems and their resolution available in the literature. In addition, by far the greatest amount of recorded information regarding actual experience with complex problems concerns those that are in the domain of public affairs, presumably because such matters are of greater general interest than the experience of individual corporations and businesses. Such experience may also be subject to greater restrictions of confidentiality. Complex decision problems are however being encountered with increasing frequency in the private sector of the economy and the characteristics of these problems arising in business and industry are increasingly aligned to those in the public domain. It is appropriate, therefore, that experience gained in dealing with complex problems in the public sector should be utilized to the greatest degree possible in considering the wider range of problems.

One of the best documented and most studied examples of the resolution of a complex decision problem is that of the Cuban Missile Crisis.[6, 7] As with many such problems, this involved two major participants, the U.S. and the U.S.S.R., and a number of participants with lesser roles such as Cuba and the European nations. The main action took place between the two major participants. Each of these participants was guided in his conduct of the affair by the deliberations of a committee that was set up specifically to deal with the crisis or that devoted most or all of its time to the problem from the time that it arose to its resolution. The frequency with which the two opposing committees met varied during the crisis, apparently according to the perceived urgency of the situation. From all recorded accounts, the agenda of the meetings of the committees on both sides were not unlike that shown in Figure 6.3.

In actual fact, most, if not all, of the actions taken by both major participants during the confrontation were concerned with imparting information or with gaining some perceived tactical advantage. Some were of a coercive structural variety, such as the dispatch by the USSR of nuclear warheads and the institution by the U.S. of the naval blockade. Others were pure communication moves, such as President Kennedy's dispatch of his family from Washington at the height of the crisis and Mr. Khrushchev's public statements about the installation of purely defensive weapons in Cuba.

The committee members on each side were apparently far from unanimous in their opinions and in their advice regarding actions that should be taken. On the U.S. side, for example, there was a considerable body of opinion that favored military action against Cuba and a countervailing group that advised a less drastic course of action. Possibly these different subgroups of the committee were playing out a hierarchically subordinate problem concerning their ascendancy as advisors to the White House while, at the same time, they participated in the resolution of the larger problem.

There were apparently a number of horizontally-linked concurrent problems that had some bearing on the resolution of the main problem. Although these problems were relatively far less important, they nonetheless had significant effects on the deliberations and the actions in the central confrontation between the U.S. and the U.S.S.R. Many of these problems concerned relationships with allies and the effects of actions (such as the US blockade) on these allies. Both sides demonstrated an awareness that their behavior in the main problem would be judged by outside observers and that these judgements might be transferred to other present and future situations as the basis for predicting likely behavior in these situations.

The conduct of the US–USSR confrontation can therefore be seen to coincide broadly with the main features of the model outlined in the previous section and illustrated in Figures 6.2, 6.4, and 6.5. The same can be said of other examples of complex problems that have arisen in the political arena in the past, such as the situation in Northern Ireland and the Arab-Israeli confrontation in the Middle East.[8] Both fit naturally into the conceptual model consisting of a series of reviews of the strategic structure of the problem by each of the participants, with structural and pure communication moves interspersed whenever those involved felt it necessary to take action to alter the available options or to impart information.

Much the same pattern of continuing review, action, and communication between participants can be detected in decision processes in a number of other areas. It is encountered, for example, in relations between corporations and government regulatory agencies, between different levels of government, within organizations operating in the private sector, and between corporations competing in the same market. In fact, any situation in which resolution of a problem can be achieved only by a process of continuing review and communication between the participants is a candidate for consideration in terms of the model illustrated in Figures 6.2, 6.4, and 6.5. This is not to say that the model is a panacea for solution of all complex decision problems. It is, rather, a general framework within which such problems can be considered and a basis from which organizational procedures to deal with such problems can be constructed.

Later in this chapter, the retrospective application of the model to the problem of siting a major facility (an airport) is described. Before this, however, it is interesting to describe a different approach to complex decision problems that provides a much less detailed model of the decision process, but one which is complementary to that described in this chapter so far.

## ISSUE MACHINES

Another model providing a general framework for the consideration of complex decision problems and having some relation to those proposed earlier is the issue machine. This model had its origin in studies of the political process. It is based on the contention that "one way . . . of looking upon a political system is to look upon it as a machine, or collection of machines, for processing issues."[9] The issue machine deals with an issue (defined as a question of choosing between alternatives) by applying certain tests to each of the alternatives. If an alternative passes the test, then it is advanced toward adoption. If it does not, it is rejected or relegated to less preferred status.

The issue machine contains a number of stations that can be compared with the participants in the model of Figure 6.4. Tests of alternatives are made at each of the stations in the machine prior to a decision regarding which alternative, if any, is to be adopted. The decision process is envisaged therefore as a run of the issue machine in which every alternative (or policy) is put through every relevant test at every station to determine its suitability for dealing with the issue. The output of the run is a set of adopted alternatives or policies or an indication that none of the alternatives is regarded as appropriate for resolution of the issue.

This method of approach to complex decision problems neglects much of the detailed content of the decision process. Factors such as the manner in which preferences for alternatives are determined and the interaction of the preferences of those involved at any given station are given little consideration in the quest for construction of a simulation of the overall working of an issue-processing system. This is acceptable only in the context of an overall view of the decision process and it is in that context that the issue machine idea bears a relation to the model discussed earlier in the text.

Suppose that the issue machine is regarded as a "black box" encompassing one complete round of consideration of a complex problem. At one face of the box the issue is fed in and, at the opposite face, the chosen policy appears. All that we know of the inside of the box is that the issue must pass by a number of stations and that the processing by these stations determines which of the policies appears at the output of the box. Suppose, further, that we are interested only in an overall view of the decision process because we have noticed that the issue concerned has been the subject of a number of attempts at resolution (or runs through the issue machine) and we are interested in comparing the results of these attempts. Note that each of the attempts may be compared to a cycle of the model depicted in Figure 6.4 containing one or more sequences of information gathering, structural evaluation, and communication. The exact number of such sequences contained in a cycle is unimportant at this time. It will become apparent in later treatment of a case history that the definition of one run through the machine or one cycle of the decision model usually becomes apparent as the actual issue under consideration is studied in detail.

Suppose that, in a particular encounter with a complex problem, each round of consideration of the issue results in the adoption of a policy. The issue machine is said to be *P-stable* if, regardless of which stations act in which sequence in each successive round, the same reasons count with the same weight for or against the alternatives and the same policy is adopted as the output of the process.[10] In other words, if, after a series of rounds of consideration of a problem, the same method of resolution is recommended regardless of which agencies back the recurrent reasons for this recommendation, the process is said to be P-stable. For example, in a broad view of the conflict in Northern Ireland there are at least four stations or participants: the British government, the Irish government, the Protestants, and the Catholics. The P-stable policy since 1920 could be said to be "partition of Ireland." This policy has remained the stable output of the decision process for over fifty years despite all the activity and despite all the resources that have been expended in the hope of resolving the problem.

It is interesting to note that P-stability apparently occurs in the Northern Ireland problem at what may well be a metaequilibrium coinciding with the conflict point. Each participant has apparently preferred the status quo at the conflict point to taking a unilateral action to move away. Furthermore, no basis has been found in negotiations over a number of years for determining to which alternative outcome a coalition of all participants should proceed in order to escape from the conflict point.

In cases such as this in which the recurrent outcome is unsatisfactory to the participants the question arises of what actions can be taken to disturb the P-stability and to bring about an outcome that is more acceptable to those involved. Appropriate actions might be in terms of: (a) the introduction of new alternatives; (b) a modification of the nature of the participants by the formation or breaking down of coalitions or by the elimination or addition of one or more; or (c) the modification of the preferences of one or more of the individual participants or the coalitions. Assuming some action of this sort were possible, even at a cost, this might be judged preferable by the participants to the alternative of another round of consideration leading to a repetition of the same outcome.

The foregoing discussion suggests four procedures that might be to the advantage of those involved in the resolution of complex decision problems:

1. early in the process of resolution a review of past problems of a similar nature should be undertaken to determine whether any exhibited P-stability and, if so, why this came about;

2. during the process of resolution and after a number of cycles of the information gathering/structural assessment/communication and negotiation sequence, the process itself should be examined for P-stability;

3. if P-stability is found to exist and the outcome is not desirable or acceptable, methods of disturbing the P-stability should be examined with a view to bringing about a more acceptable outcome;

4. on the other hand, if a P-stable situation is desirable and acceptable, methods of reinforcing the stability should be examined.

The issue machine idea provides, therefore, some guidelines that are appropriate for those considering the strategic structure of a complex decision problem. It suggests also that it would be advantageous to reconstruct the past history of a current problem in terms of the continuing model of Figures 6.4 and 6.5 to determine which of the information gathering/structural evaluation/communication cycles of the model may be considered together to constitute a round of an issue machine. Furthermore, it may well be advantageous to use the same procedure as the process of dealing with the problem unfolds. These thoughts are carried into the discussion of a case history in the next section.

## An Illustrative Case History

Many of the characteristics of the models of complex decision processes that have just been discussed can be illustrated by reference to a case history. The purpose of such illustration is not to suggest that the resolution of each problem of this nature rigidly conforms to a model that is, at best, only a general representation of the actual process. The purpose is, rather, to point out features of the problem and of the resolution process that are similar to those incorporated in the general model, and to suggest methods based on actual experience by which these features can be recognized in a future encounter with a problem that is new and seemingly completely different. The danger in writing a case history of this sort is that the overuse of hindsight will result in conclusions that are less valid than would be desired. This pitfall will be avoided to the greatest extent possible in the following narrative. In addition, only sufficient detail will be presented to serve the purposes of illustration and the emphasis throughout will be on the broad outlines of the problem.

The problem chosen for illustration concerns the selection of a site for a second Toronto airport. This problem aroused a great deal of public controversy in the time period from 1967 until 1975. It began when the Canadian (Federal) government announced that a new airport would be necessary to meet the anticipated future demand for air travel. It ended, at least temporarily, when plans for a new airport were abandoned in 1975.

The situation had, from the start, many of the characteristics that are common to complex decision problems. For example, all participants had only limited information concerning the elements of the problem. Despite the fact that a second airport was already under construction outside Montreal and despite information available from similar projects at Washington (Dulles) and Paris (Charles de Gaulle), only partial information was available to the planners concerning the factors that might affect the selection of a site. Very little detailed weather and environmental data were available relative to possible sites. Projections of demand for air travel in and out of Toronto were based on extrapolation of past trends and on the continuation of existing economic conditions. Little information was available on the reaction of those who might become involved in the decision process at each possible site or on their attitudes and preferences for or against a new airport in their neighborhood.

In common with many other complex decision problems, there were a number of participants involved in the process of resolution. First among these was the Federal government, which has the responsibility for building and maintaining major airport facilities and, more generally, for providing facilities to meet the demand for air transportation. Second, the Ontario government was a participant by virtue of the fact that the airport would be built in areas within its jurisdiction and would require services such as roads and sewers that fell under its general responsibility. In addition, the Provincial government has the responsibility for urban planning and development, and for preservation of the environment and ecology of the province. It had already published a Toronto-centered Region Plan in which these matters were discussed in detail. Other participants can be identified only tentatively in the early stages of the problem. However, it was clear from the beginning that local politicians, local contractors, local citizens' groups, local governments, the airlines, and the federal and provincial opposition parties might have some part to play in the resolution. Each of these participants no doubt had their individual sets of objectives and values that ultimately led them to express preferences for alternatives. In addition, a multitude of relationships existed between the participants as a result of participation in previous decision problems or other similar activities or by virtue of their being involved in other concurrent problem situations.

From the start, the action space of the problem was relatively well defined and was restricted primarily to the factors involved in choosing a site. Linkages to concurrent problems appeared to be weak. Effects on related problems that might be caused by the selection of any particular site were thought to be capable of speedy resolution. This had, in fact, been the case in the selection of the site for the second Montreal airport and in its construction. There was little reason to believe at the start that the experience would not be similar for the Toronto airport.

A large number of technical studies were made of the factors comprising the environment of the problem and particularly of the technological aspects that might impose constraints on the selection of sites.[11] These studies were mainly commissioned by the Federal and Provincial Governments and appear to have been as objective as is possible in the circumstances in which they were undertaken. As is usually the case, however, they provided only partial information on the technological factors involved in airport location. In addition, they were inevitably incomplete. For example, at one stage of the decision process a local group with minimal resources was able to produce data on weather conditions in an area being considered as a site and to make considerable play of the fact that the government proponents of the site had not collected or studied such information.

Perhaps the most significant factor in the area of technical studies was the fact that forecasts of demand for passenger and cargo air transportation were based on extrapolations of data relating to a period in the 1960s that was characterized by great economic expansion and major increases in real disposable income. Both these factors had resulted in an air traffic boom and in large increases in the demand for airport facilities. Planners foresaw a continuation of these trends and forecast an exponential growth of air travel in the foreseeable future. They did not foresee the energy crisis and the recession of the early 1970s that contributed to a levelling off of the demand for air travel. To be fair, nor did most other people at the time. This factor was to have a major effect on the decision process as it unfolded. The lesson to be learned is that, wherever possible, the sensitivity of conclusions to variations in assumptions and analysis should be assessed, however unlikely these variations are felt to be at the time. It is not likely that anyone would have given credence to a suggestion in 1967 that air travel demand would level off or that the thrust towards a new airport would have been modified in any way. Nevertheless, events showed the error of the extrapolation and made a mockery of the assumption of the inevitability of expansion of the demand for air travel.

In summary, the selection of the airport site involved a number of participants with different interests and there were a number of objectives to be achieved. Fulfillment of one objective might well result in underachievement of another. No participant had complete information that would allow construction of a comprehensive model of the situation and solution by a well-understood analytical method. The total information available to any one participant was not necessarily the same as that in the possession of any other. Their perceptions of the problem were subjective and to some extent different. Much of the information that was central to the consideration of the problem was uncertain because it consisted of extrapolation of past trends and data into the future. While much information and experience of a general and technical nature could be drawn from other encounters with similar site selection problems, many important features of the Toronto airport situation were particular to the local area so that the problem was essentially new and unique. The decision involved substantial commitments of funds and installation of major facilities, so that once construction at a selected site had been started, the decision would be progressively more difficult to reverse as time went on. Furthermore, the problem was linked to other coexisting ones in which some or all of the same participants were involved and in which repercussions of any decision or action regarding selection of a site for the airport might be felt. The problem therefore exhibited most of the characteristics described in the first and second chapters of this text.

*The First Round—Expansion of the Existing Malton Airport*

The first round in the (reconstructed) Toronto airport decision problem concerned the possibility of expanding the facilities at the Toronto International Airport at Malton. This airport is to the north-west of the city and is rapidly becoming surrounded by urban and industrial development. On the basis of estimates of passenger and cargo traffic made in 1967 the existing facilities at Malton could be shown to be rapidly approaching saturation. A plan was prepared for expanding the capacity of this airport, calling for addition of 3,000 acres of land to the site and the installation of new runways and associated facilities. The enlarged airport would have required additional access roads and other services and would have been expected to attract additional light industry and service oriented facilities to the area. This, in turn, would have resulted in further urban development in an area that was already one of very rapid growth, compared, for example, to the area northeast of the city.

The Province in its plan for development of the entire region had already noted the rapid growth to the west and northwest of Toronto and had pointed out that this might result in undesirable congestion if allowed to proceed unchecked. It recommended diversion of urban development to the northeast and east of the city wherever this was possible. Although this plan was published and the other participants, particularly the Federal Government, were clearly aware of its contents, it is not clear what impact it had on the thinking of those involved at the time.

Other participants in this round of the problem were: the Metro Toronto Council, the Local (Mississauga) Council, a Citizens' Protest group, and the airlines. It seems, however, that these participants had little power to influence the outcome. They exercised what power they had mainly in support of the Provincial Government's opposition to the expansion of the airport and facilities at Malton.

It is interesting to consider the situation as representatives of the Federal Government might have done at the time and to describe it in the form of an analysis of options. This attempt to reconstruct a situation comprising many different interests and their various interactions several years after the event is inevitably very broad and may exclude details that many think were vital to the problem. However, the objective here is to illustrate the application of a model and a way of thinking about a problem rather than to achieve absolute historical accuracy. Care has been taken to ensure that the details given are drawn from the available documentation of the case. No distortion of the facts has been included knowingly in preparing this account.

The participants in this round and their available courses of action might have been listed as in Table 6.1 by a representative of the Federal Government in a first attempt at assessing the strategic structure of the problem. As part of his investigation, he would no doubt have been interested in the stability of the outcome in which a completely new airport was built, so this is shown as the particular scenario to be investigated. Scenarios considered to be infeasible are shown at the right-hand side of the Table. Minor participants are shown lumped into one labelled "Others" because their influence at this stage is relatively small.

The Federal Government might have considered that it had unilateral improvements and scenarios that were not preferred relative to the particular scenario (build new airport) as shown in Table 6.2. Reasoning behind selection of the scenario (Column 1) shown as "preferred" to the building of a new airport might have been that it would be cheaper and quicker to expand the facilities at Malton than to construct an entirely new airport at a new site. Expanding Malton would have provided a short-term (incremental) solution and would have given time to consider further action in the light of new information as it became available. A scenario in which neither Malton was expanded nor a new airport built (Column 3) was probably not preferred in the light of the government's responsibility to provide facilities for air travel and in view of the criticism that would arise if these facilities were not provided. A scenario in which a new airport was to be built but the decision postponed for a while (Column 4) was probably attractive, but may have been eventually not preferred in view of the rapid increase in demand for air travel that was forecast at the time.

Sanctions against the Federal Government taking the unilateral improvement shown in Column 1 of Table 6.2 (expand Malton rather than build a new airport) are shown in Table 6.3. These sanctions consisted entirely of actions by the other participants actively to oppose the expansion of Malton rather than cooperate or not oppose this course of action. The extent to which the Federal Government was deterred from proceeding with a plan to expand the facilities at Malton was no doubt dependent on the credibility of these sanctions. This was dependent in turn on the power of the opposing participants to influence the outcome and on the negotiation, bargaining, and communication between the participants during the course of the round. Few details are available of any negotiations that took place between

Table 6.1   PARTICIPANTS AND AVAILABLE COURSES OF ACTION (OPTIONS)
IN THE MALTON EXPANSION ROUND

| Participants | Available Courses of Action | Particular Scenario to be Investigated | Infeasibles |
|---|---|---|---|
| Federal Government | Expand Malton | 0 | 1 |
| | Postpone decision | 0 | |
| | Find new site | 1 | 1 |
| Provincial Government | Cooperate with federal government | 1 | 1 |
| | Actively oppose federal government | 0 | 1 |
| Others (Metro Council, Local Council, Citizens, Airlines) | Cooperate with federal government | 1 | 1 |
| | Actively oppose federal government | 0 | 1 |
| | Cooperate with provincial Government | – | 1 |
| | Actively oppose provincial Government | – | 1 |

Table 6.2   Unilateral Improvements for the Federal Government
from the Particular Scenario (Build New Airport)

| | Available Courses of Action | Preferred | Particular Scenario | Not Preferred | |
|---|---|---|---|---|---|
| Federal Government | Expand Malton | 1 | 0 | 0 | 0 |
| | Postpone decision | −(1) | 0 | −(1) | 1 |
| | Find new site | 0 | 1 | 0 | 1 |
| | Column Number | 1 | 2 | 3 | 4 |

the participants. In the actual event, the Federal Government did not take the course of action shown in Table 6.1 as a unilateral improvement. This may have been due to sanctions by the other participants. On the other hand, it may have been because representatives of the Federal Government did not, in fact, prefer the Malton expansion to the building of a new airport. This we do not know, nor is there a record of any hierarchically linked, subordinate problem in which factions within the major participants may have vied for prevalence of their views. The course of action "Build New Airport" emerged as the outcome of this round and attention was concentrated on the selection of a site.

### The Second Round—Beeton Flats and Orangeville

As soon as the abandonment of plans to expand Malton was announced, local politicians in a number of areas became interested in the possibility that the site for the new airport might be selected in their locality. Some saw advantage in such an outcome and took steps to promote sites in their area. Notable examples of this activity took place at two locations both within 40 to 50 miles of Toronto and to the northwest. These locations were Beeton Flats and Orangeville. These sites were promoted almost simultaneously (but by different groups) and the play was broadly the same in the two cases. Details and individual activities were, of course, different, but this does not preclude the treating of both cases as one round in this survey.

The major participants in the second round were again the Federal and Provincial Governments. Their available courses of action were essentially the same as in the Malton Expansion round, as is shown in Table 6.4. The "Expand Malton" course of action by the Federal

Table 6.3    Sanctions Against a Unilateral Improvement by the Federal Government (Expand Malton)

| Participants | Available Courses of Action | Preferred | Particular Scenario | Not Preferred |
|---|---|---|---|---|
| Federal Government | Expand Malton | | 0 | 1 |
| | Postpone decision | | 0 | -(1) |
| | Find new site | | 1 | 0 |
| Provincial Government | Cooperate with Federal Government | | 1 | 0 |
| | Actively oppose Federal Government | | 0 | 1 |
| Others (Metro Council, Local Council, Citizens, Airlines) | Cooperate with Federal Government | | 1 | 0 |
| | Actively oppose Federal Government | | 0 | 1 |
| | Cooperate with Provincial Government | | – | -(0) |
| | Actively oppose Provincial Government | | – | -(1) |

Table 6.4  PARTICIPANTS AND AVAILABLE COURSES OF ACTIONS IN
THE SECOND (BEETON FLATS/ORANGEVILLE) ROUND

| Participants | Available Courses of Action | Particular Scenario |
|---|---|---|
| Federal Government | Build at Beeton Flats/Orangeville | 0 |
|  | Postpone decision | 0 |
|  | Find new site | 1 |
| Provincial Government | Cooperate with Federal Government | 1 |
|  | Actively oppose Federal Government | 0 |
| Local Politicians | Cooperate with Federal Government | 1 |
|  | Actively oppose Federal Government | 0 |
|  | Cooperate with Provincial Government | – |
|  | Actively oppose Provincial Government | – |
| Local Citizens and Airlines | Cooperate with Federal Government | 1 |
|  | Actively oppose Federal Government | 0 |
|  | Cooperate with Provincial Government | – |
|  | Actively oppose Provincial Government | – |

Government has been replaced at this stage by "Build at Beeton Flats/Orangeville." The structure of this participant's options was, however, essentially unchanged. The basic choices were to build at a particular site, build at another site, or postpone the decision. However, participants that played a minor role in the Malton round split into two groups and took a far more active part in this round. The local politicians promoted their local site and another group (primarily local citizens and the airlines) opposed it for various and different reasons.

The Federal Government, in its search for a site, was presumably still interested in whether the scenario represented by "Find New Site" was stable or whether that shown as "Build at Beeton Flats/

Orangeville" was an improvement against which there were no sanctions or against which the possible sanctions were not sufficiently credible to deter the choice of one or other of these sites.

Reproduction of the various analysis of options tables to represent this round of the problem is not necessary to the continuity of this discussion. Testing of whether the scenario of "Building at Beeton Flats/Orangeville" is an improvement over the "Find New Site" particular scenario of Table 6.4 is found to depend on the credibility of sanctions by the Provincial Government and by the Local Citizens and Airlines in opposition to the Beeton Flats or Orangeville Sites. In the event, these sanctions prevailed and the particular scenario "Find New Site" was found to be stable in the second round as in the first. Why this occurred is difficult to say. It may have been that the Federal Government was not particularly interested in the Beeton Flats/Orangeville sites and was participating in this round in order to appear to be responding to the views of local groups. On the other hand, the opposition of the local citizens and the airlines may have been the prime factor.

The round is noteworthy by virtue of a number of features. First, despite the fact that the site under discussion was different, that many of the detailed factors were different, and that the minor participants were made up of groups with different compositions and interests, P-stability was demonstrated between the first two rounds in terms of the outcome requiring search for a new site. Second, whereas the first round was conducted primarily between two major participants, in the second round participants such as Local Politicians, Local Citizens, and Airlines played an important part. Local Citizens of Beeton Flats and Orangeville (citizens groups in both areas were opposed to an airport in their neighborhood) spent considerable time and resources on steps designed to increase their power to influence the outcome. The Orangeville group produced evidence of unfavorable weather conditions in the area (as compared to Malton) that fostered an implicit coalition between the group and the airlines. This may have been the basis of a credible sanction against the sites in that area. On the other hand, the sanction of the Provincial Government against a site so far from Toronto and in an essentially agricultural and recreational area may have been the most important.

### The Third Round—Pickering

At this point (and possibly before), the Federal Government was apparently convinced that the best hope for selecting a site was to form a coalition with the Provincial Government. This was appar-

ently done, and on March 2, 1972 both governments announced a
decision to build a new airport at Pickering. They revealed an "Annex
of Understanding" giving details of the cooperation agreed upon to
bring the project to completion. The announcement was a surprise
to all other participants. Notice was given that expropriation procedures for an 18,000 acre site were to start immediately. The Federal-
Provincial Government coalition apparently regarded themselves and
their decision as invincible. Both were strong (majority) governments
and the feeling of invincibility was perhaps reinforced when the Federal Government was returned with a large majority in an election in
July 1972 in which the choice of the site at Pickering did not become
a major issue. Selection of Pickering appeared to be a guaranteed
improvement for the coalition of Federal and Provincial Governments,
against which there were no credible sanctions. P-stability at the
"Find New Site" outcome had apparently been broken by formation
of the coalition and by the disarray of the opposition caused by the
surprise announcement of an apparent *fait accompli.*

Two major factors were at work, however, that were to change the
situation significantly. First, two quasi-natural events that can be
described as "Recession" and "Energy Crisis" had occurred. These
events were just beginning to affect the problem of choice of an airport site. Recession had the effect of decreasing the amount of disposable income available to current and potential users of air travel
and reducing the demand for air freight as a method of distribution
of goods. The energy crisis had the more permanent effect of increasing the cost of air services due to the major increase in the price of
the necessary fuel. Both these events caused the demand for air services to drop significantly and made the previous estimates of future
demand appear to be far too high.

The second major new factor was the emergence of a persistent
and well-organized citizens' group in opposition to the airport at
Pickering. This group was called "People or Planes" (or POP). It
fought the airport by all legitimate means, ridiculed government statements that it would have "minimal environmental impact" when
15,000 acres of prime farmland would be lost. It sought injunctions
to delay construction and expropriation of land, called for an impartial
Commission of Inquiry, and enlisted the aid of political parties in
opposition to the Federal and Provincial Governments. All these activities were designed to increase the power of the group to influence
the outcome.

At this stage, the situation can be described broadly in terms of the
analysis of options tableaux shown in Tables 6.5 and 6.6. Table 6.5
shows a unilateral improvement for the Federal-Provincial Govern-

Table 6.5 Unilateral Improvements for the Federal-Provincial Government Coalition from "Build at Another Site" Scenario

| | Available Courses of Action | Preferred | Particular Scenario | Not Preferred | Infeasible |
|---|---|---|---|---|---|
| Federal-Provincial | Build at Pickering | 1 | 0 | 0 | 1 |
| Government Coalition | Postpone decision | 0 | 0 | – | 1 |
| | Build at another site | 0 | 1 | – | 1 |

175

ment coalition in terms of building the airport at Pickering. This was preferred by the coalition to the previously P-stable scenario of selecting a site other than the one under consideration at the time.

Table 6.6 shows sanctions by the other participants against this unilateral improvement by the coalition. In this table, quasi-natural events are shown as options of Nature. The question of whether the sanctions shown (or any combination of them) would have deterred the Federal-Provincial Government coalition from proceeding with plans for the Pickering airport depended on the perception by the coalition of the credibility and effectiveness of the sanctions. In the early days following the announcement of the selection of the site and the "Annex of Understanding" between the governments, it is apparent that the possible sanctions did not deter the coalition. The governments were secure in their plan to press on with construction of the airport.

There followed a period of intensive negotiation, bargaining, and communication between the participants. Structural moves in this period included: (a) sending of bulldozers to break ground as a symbolic start of construction; (b) barring of residents from expropriated property; (c) occupation of such property by protest groups; (d) setting up a Commission of Inquiry (possibly as an attempt by the Federal Government to appear to have considered all points of view); and (e) application by POP for an injunction to prevent the Inquiry Commission from making its report on the grounds of alleged conflict of interest with respect to one of its members. The period was noteworthy also in terms of a wide variety of pure communication moves by all the participants. As a result of this activity, however, the strategic structure of the situation as it was probably perceived by the coalition still showed no credible sanctions against the improvement represented by building the airport at Pickering.

The stability of this outcome was broken abruptly in September 1975 by another quasi-natural event—the result of the Provincial election that left the government of the Province in a weak (minority) position. Determined opposition by the other political parties was a major threat to the government retaining power. One of the first acts of the newly weakened Provincial Government was to break the coalition by refusing to provide services to the site at Pickering. The Federal Government had no option other than to cease construction at the new airport. People or Planes celebrated what they saw as a great victory.

In actual fact, the Provincial election was probably the factor that allowed the government participants to move away from positions about which they had become increasingly uneasy. A great deal of

Table 6.6  SANCTIONS AGAINST THE UNILATERAL IMPROVEMENTS BY
THE FEDERAL-PROVINCIAL GOVERNMENT COALITION

| Available Courses of Action | Preferred | Particular Scenario | Not Preferred |
|---|---|---|---|
| **Federal-Provincial Government Coalition** | | | |
| Build at Pickering | 1 | 0 | |
| Postpone decision | 0 | 0 | |
| Build at another site | 0 | 1 | |
| **People or Planes** | | | |
| Employ delaying tactics | | | 1 – |
| Seek coalition with opposition | | | – 1 |
| **Opposition Political Parties** | | | |
| Support people or planes | | | 1 |
| **Nature** | | | |
| Recession | | | 1 – |
| Energy crisis | | | – 1 |
| Column Number | 1 | 2 | 3 4 5 6 7 |
| | ↑ Unilateral improvement | ↑ Previous P-stable scenario | ↑ Possible sanctions |

evidence was being published to the effect that the new airport was unnecessary. In the changed circumstances of 1975, similar projects in other countries were being regarded by many as white elephants. Also, costs were escalating and the era of grandiose plans seemed to be past, at least for the time being. These factors may well have eroded support for the position of the governments in the broader situation, by virtue of the results of hierarchically subordinate situations within the two major participants. The reduction in demand for air travel caused by the recession and energy crisis may have strengthened the hand of those opposed to the new airport within the Federal and Provincial Governments. These events may have caused other coexisting and linked problems to appear to have greater urgency and priority for available funds.

Whatever the detailed reasons for the events, the situation at the end of Round 3 must have appeared to representatives of the Federal Government much as shown in Table 6.7. In this table, (Column 1), the new course of action "Do Nothing" is seen as a guaranteed improvement from the continuation of the search for a site (Column 2) for all participants, at least for the time being.

### The Strategic Structure of the Problem

The strategic structure of the problem can be illustrated by a diagram as in Figure 6.6. In this diagram, the action emanates from the scenario "Find New Site" shown just to the left of center. Round 1 consists of the loop to the top left, resulting in the scenario "Find New Site" being stable. Round 2 is similar and is shown to the bottom left. Round 3 is to the right of center. The improvement for the coalition of Federal and Provincial Governments leads to the solution "Pickering," against which there are no credible sanctions until the result of the Provincial election (a quasi-natural event) intervenes. This leads to the breakup of the coalition resulting in a conflict point. The improvement from the conflict point for all participants is the new option for the Federal Government "Do Nothing," which may of course be a version of the original "Postpone Decision" alternative.

### Points Illustrated by the Case History

The purpose of recounting this case history has been to illustrate how the models of complex decision problems described earlier in

Table 6.7   The Situation at the End of Round Three
(As Probably Seen by Federal Government Representatives)

| Participants | Available Courses of Action | Preferred | Particular Scenario | Not Preferred | | Infeasibles | | | |
|---|---|---|---|---|---|---|---|---|---|
| Federal Government | Build at Pickering | 0 | 0 | 1 | 0 | 1 | 1 | – | 0 |
| | Postpone decision | – | 0 | – | 1 | – | – | – | – |
| | Build at another site | 0 | 1 | 0 | 1 | 1 | – | 1 | 0 |
| | Do nothing | 1 | 0 | 0 | 0 | 0 | 1 | 1 | 0 |
| Provincial Government | Cooperate with Federal Government | – | 0 | 0 | – | | | | |
| | Actively oppose Federal Government | – | 0 | 1 | – | | | | |
| Others (local Councils, Citizens, Airlines) | Cooperate with Federal Government | – | 0 | 0 | 0 | | | | |
| | Actively oppose Federal Government | – | 0 | 0 | 0 | | | | |
| | Cooperate with Provincial Government | – | – | – | – | | | | |
| | Actively oppose Provincial Government | – | – | – | – | | | | |
| Nature | Recession | 1 | 1 | 1 | 1 | | | | |
| | Energy crisis | 1 | 1 | 1 | 1 | | | | |
| | Column number | 1 | 2 | 3 | 4 | 5 | 6 | 7 | 8 |

179

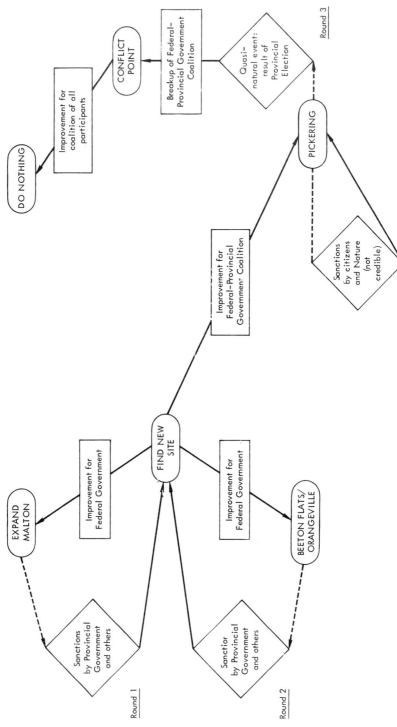

**Figure 6.6** *Strategic Structure of the Airport Site Selection Problem*

this chapter can be utilized to investigate and explore their characteristics. The following summary of points illustrated by the case history is interesting in considering the applicability and usefulness of the models:

- the dependence of the outcome on the interaction of preferences and attitudes of a number of participants;
- the frailty of estimates of future values of important factors and parameters (such as the demand for air travel) and the need for maintaining these estimates current in the light of possible changes in conditions;
- the incompleteness of the information available to the participants and the fact that each participant's information may be different from that of the others;
- the natural division of the problem into a number of rounds and the illustration of P-stability over the first two rounds;
- the importance of coalitions, their formation, and dissolution in the decision process and the related need for considering them in the analysis of complex problems;
- the tendency of participants to favor short-term (incremental) solutions such as the extension of existing facilities at Malton rather than the construction of a completely new site;
- the importance of considering sanctions that may apply against courses of action (even those of powerful participants) and also of considering the credibility of these sanctions;
- the different modes of communication in the negotiation and bargaining phase of each round, ranging from surprise announcements (in the case of Pickering) to open meetings between participants;
- the use of both pure communication and structural moves in negotiations and bargaining;
- the important effect of natural and quasi-natural events on the decision process and the related need to consider these events in the analysis of complex decision problems.

### SUMMARY

Resolution of a complex decision problem is sometimes undertaken cooperatively by those involved if they adhere to the same objectives and have the same value systems. In many cases, however, the participants in a complex problem have different interests and values. Resolution of the problem in such circumstances must be as a result of the interaction of the participants. The outcome depends on their relative power to influence the decision process. If one participant is relatively much more powerful, the responsibility for determining the outcome may lie entirely with that participant. If two or more participants are of roughly equal power, resolution of the problem can be achieved only by a process of negotiation and bargaining between them.

Each participant has subjective perceptions of the number of others involved in the problem, their characteristics, and their power to influence the problem. Each participant also has perceptions of the action space of the problem, the linkages to other problems, the characteristics of the environment of the problem, the constraints on courses of action, and the possibility of occurrence of future natural and quasi-natural events. In addition, each has perceptions of the perceptions of the other participants concerning these factors.

A participant involved in a complex decision problem must openly or implicitly undertake three phases of activity in the process of resolution: (a) gathering and review of information and postulation of alternative future scenarios, (b) assessment of the strategic structure of the problem based on the available information and, (c) exchange of information with the other participants during negotiations or bargaining. The relative importance, duration, and content of these phases depends on the nature of the problem. Resolution of the problem seldom involves a single run through these phases in sequence. The tendency is for continual review of the problem resulting in a number of cycles through the component phases of the process of resolution as events unfold. This is consistent with actual experience and practice in dealing with these problems, with strategies such as incrementalism and fractionating, and with the need for adaptation and learning in activities such as organizational planning and policy making.

A model of the decision process can be constructed based on the above ideas. It consists of a continual series of activities in the three phases. Information and perceptions resulting from data gathering and analysis are utilized in the consideration of the strategic structure of the problem. The agenda of these strategic evaluation sessions consists of a review of available information and previous evaluations, followed by a reassessment of the strategic structure and decisions regarding any actions that must be taken at the time. The nature of the information to be imparted to the other participants must be decided here, as well as the means by which such information is to be conveyed. An elaboration of the model representing one decision problem includes an illustration of the linkages to other coexisting problems, both vertical (hierarchical) and horizontal. One of the most important types of vertically linked problems concerns those that are internal to a participant involved in a problem at a higher level. These vertically linked problems occur often in organizations and communities where internal matters affect the position taken on behalf of the organization in a problem in a wider field.

The continuous model described above can be related to the idea of issue machines. In this broad concept, the whole process of dealing with a complex problem is looked upon as though it were a machine for treating issues. The issue machine consists of a number of stations (participants) that test alternative courses of action or policies according to certain standards of acceptability. The output of the run is a set of adopted policies or alternatives for resolution of the issue. This output is said to be P-stable if, regardless of which stations act in which sequence in each successive round of consideration, the same reasons count with the same weight for or against the alternatives and the same policy is adopted as the output of the process. P-stability has been demonstrated in some complex problems over a number of years, as in the persistence of the partition alternative in Northern Ireland, for example. It is of interest to consider what might disturb P-stability, if it exists. In this way, an undesirable outcome that has persisted over a number of rounds might be changed.

The model of the treatment of a complex decision problem contained in this chapter can be seen to apply to a number of actual cases. Most of the best known of those that can be used for illustration are in the field of international politics. However, on closer scrutiny many problems in other areas can be seen to fit the same model. For example, problems of industrial relations and of the siting of major facilities can be represented in this manner.

## DISCUSSION TOPICS

1. Each participant in a complex decision problem has a set of perceptions of the perceptions of the other participants. What is the importance of this factor in resolution of these problems and how should the approach of any one participant be affected by it?

2. Is the resolution of complex decision problems necessarily a continuous process? Are such problems ever solved? What is the link between the idea of a continuous process of resolution and incrementalism?

3. Is contingency planning essentially the same thing as a continuous process of decision making?

4. How well, in your opinion, does the model illustrated in Figure 6.1 represent the manner in which complex decision problems are handled in organizations? What are the deficiencies of the model or of present procedures in organizations?
5. Do you agree with the distinction between assessment of the strategic structure of a problem and the communication, negotiation and bargaining phase of resolution? Is it useful to separate these conceptually and, if so, why?
6. How can the relationships between the various interests within a participant affect that participant's behavior in a linked problem? What bearing do your conclusions have on the manner in which positions to be taken on behalf of an organization should be formulated?
7. Do you think experience with complex decision problems in national and international politics is transferable to other fields, such as intercorporate problems or government-business relations? If not, why not? If so, what are the problems that might be experienced in such a transfer?
8. Is the concept of issue machines helpful in considering complex decision problems? What are its strengths and weaknesses in this connection?
9. Does P-stability always occur at a metaequilibrium?
10. Are complex problems met in actual experience likely to be resolved in a number of rounds as suggested by the issue machine idea?
11. How would you use the models described in this chapter to design procedures for treating complex decision problems in your organization?
12. Do these models coincide with the intuitive methods of treatment on which successful managers rely? If not, what are the differences and similarities and how should the models be changed to take account of them?

## REFERENCES

1. Etzioni, Amatai. *The Active Society*. New York: The Free Press, 1968, p. 287.
2. Fisher, Roger. "Fractionating Conflict," In *International Conflict and Behavioral Science*, edited by Roger Fisher. New York: Basic Books, 1964, pp. 91–109.
3. Braybrooke, D., and C. E. Lindblom. *A Strategy of Decision*. New York: The Free Press, 1963, pp. 99–104.

4. Popper, Karl R. *The Open Society and Its Enemies,* vol. 1. Princeton, N.J.: Princeton University Press, 1960, pp. 155–60.
5. Ackoff, R. L. *Redesigning the Future.* New York: John Wiley & Sons, 1974, pp. 29–32.
6. Allison, G. T. "Conceptual Models of the Cuban Missile Crisis." *American Political Science Review,* 63 (September 1969): 689–718. See also Allison's *Essence of Decision,* Little Brown, 1971.
7. Janis, I. L. *Victims of Group-Think* Boston, Mass.: Houghton Mifflin Company, 1972, Chapter 6.
8. See for example, J. E. Dougherty and R. L. Pfaltzgraff. *Contending Theories of International Relations.* Philadelphia: J. B. Lippincott Company, 1971, pp. 337–40, concerning the outbreak of World War I, and J. G. Stoessinger. *Why Nations Go To War.* New York: St. Martins Press, 1974.
9. Braybrooke, D. *Traffic Congestion Goes Through the Issue Machine.* London: Routledge & Kegan Paul, Ltd., 1974.
10. Ibid., p. 21.
11. For example, P. H. Beinhaker, "Airport Location and Terminal Systems." In *Readings in Airport Planning.* Department of Civil Engineering, University of Toronto, Toronto, Ontario.

# 7
# Organizational Procedures for Dealing with Complex Decision Problems

## INTRODUCTION

The preceding chapters have been concerned with three phases in the process of resolution of a complex decision problem and with the relationship between them in an overall model of the process. In the course of the discussion, a number of methods and techniques have been described that are found useful by participants in practical encounters with complex decision problems. It now remains to relate this model and the associated methods and techniques to existing organizational functions and procedures and to suggest how they can be incorporated into the day-to-day work of modern organizations in government, business, and community affairs.

The model and the techniques proposed earlier in the text for dealing with complex decision problems are sufficiently broad and flexible to be appropriate for use in a wide range of decision situations. They are based in large part on actual experience in dealing with these problems. Furthermore, they have been designed to take account of the major characteristics of complex problems that have been encountered in a large number of practical situations.

Nevertheless, the model of the process of resolution of complex decision problems described in Chapter 6 is, at best, only an artificial representation of the real thing. It cannot be said to simulate accurately all aspects of the interaction between the participants and between them and the environment. Many assumptions and simplifications have been made in the attempt to reduce an intricate and complex process to a simple succession of steps that can be readily explained and understood. The majority of these assumptions and simplifications have been made in areas concerned with the behavior of the participants and with the nature of the interaction between the individuals involved. These are areas in which great care must be taken not to draw too great a generalization from the limited amount of descriptive material that is available.

Managers and administrators usually base their practical approaches to complex decision problems on intuition derived from long experience of the behavior of those involved. It would be foolish, therefore, to suggest that existing methods should be discarded completely in favor of those associated with an artificial model of the process. A much more tenable suggestion is that the model be used to provide a basic structure into which a variety of practical procedures for resolution of complex decision problems can be incorporated. In this way, the body of descriptive material on which the model is based can act as an underpinning for procedures proposed for use in actual encounters with complex problems while, at the same time, allowing freedom for those involved to use such intuition, judgement, and practical experience as they think appropriate. Organizational procedures derived in this manner are likely to be unobtrusive and much less restrictive to managers and administrators. On the other hand, the structuring provided by the model is likely to make practical procedures more efficient and to reduce repetition in execution of the various activities required. Those involved are likely to gain assurance from the existence of a logical backing to their work. They can derive confidence from the use of procedures that ensure that important aspects of the problem are not being overlooked.

## ACTIVITIES INVOLVED IN THE RESOLUTION OF COMPLEX DECISION PROBLEMS

The activities that must be undertaken in each of the phases of resolution of a complex decision problem and the aims and objectives of these activities are summarized in Table 7.1. Some of these activities are similar to those involved in the functions of planning and policy making and in the handling of external contacts in many

Table 7.1   ACTIVITIES, AIMS AND OBJECTIVES IN THE THREE PHASES OF THE PROCESS OF RESOLUTION OF COMPLEX DECISION PROBLEMS

| Phase | Activities | Aims and Objectives |
|---|---|---|
| 1. Perception and Formulation | (a) data gathering and review | (a) greatest possible variety of pertinent information considered |
| | (b) problem perception | (b) continual review of own perceptions of participants and environment |
| | (c) formulation of possible courses of action | (c) continual review of other participants' possible perceptions |
| | (d) perception of possible outcomes and of preferences between them | (d) avoidance of phenomena such as "group-think" and suppression of negative information |
| | | (e) retention of flexibility of options and continual addition of new alternatives |
| 2. Strategic Analysis | (a) assessment of the strategic structure of the problem and of future scenarios that might be stable | (a) to provide an indication of possible future outcomes as a basis for immediate or future action |
| | (b) assessment of the effect of any time-dependencies on the strategic structure and on future possibly stable scenarios | (b) to determine how the strategic structure may be changed by possible future actions and events |
| | (c) conduct of sensitivity testing of the analysis | (c) to assess how the results of analysis might vary with changes in assumptions |
| | (d) choice of tactics to be used in interaction with other participants | |
| 3. Communication, Negotiation and Bargaining | (a) imparting of information to other participants and gathering of information from them | (a) achievement of a more preferred (rather than a less preferred) outcome |
| | | (b) to obtain information for use in succeeding considerations of the problem |

existing organizations. A basic difference, however, is that most conventional decision-making activities are related to operational and administrative decisions concerned with the efficient and effective use of resources and with the formal structures by which the organization functions. It contrast to these essentially internal matters, complex decision problems are concerned with strategic (and primarily external) issues, involving relationships between the organization and other participants in the problem and between the organization and its environment. The detailed nature of the work of resolving complex decision problems is, therefore, very different. There is, for example, a greater emphasis in data gathering on matters external to the organization and a lesser interest in data that is accumulated primarily for monitoring the organization's internal functions. In the same manner, communications arising from the decision making process tend to be more with individuals and entities outside the organization rather than within it. The question arises, therefore, of whether the resolution of complex decision problems should be undertaken by the same parts of the organization that are concerned with internal management and control or whether a new and separate unit should be set up within the organization specifically to deal with these problems.

## RESPONSIBILITY WITHIN ORGANIZATIONS
## FOR RESOLUTION OF
## COMPLEX DECISION PROBLEMS

Resolution of a complex decision problem is often made the responsibility of a team or task force made up of personnel from the various divisions of an organization. This unit is constituted especially to deal with a particular problem. It operates outside the normal lines of authority and usually reports to the senior manager or administrator responsible for the decision. It can, however, draw on the resources of the organization for information and assistance.

The task force approach has many advantages. Members are able to concentrate on the problem at hand and on any others to which it is linked, without the distraction of the day-to-day responsibilities of their usual jobs. Teams normally work with a higher degree of cooperation and harmony. The opportunity for dynamic leadership is most freely available in a team concentrating on a single purpose. The likelihood of interpersonal and intergroup rivalries is much less in such circumstances. A working atmosphere that is unrestricted by previous routine and work habits is also conducive to creative activity and to the introduction of innovative methods of dealing with complex problems.

There are, however, some disadvantages to the treatment of complex problems by small cohesive groups that have been dealt with at length by Janis in his treatment of the group-think phenomenon. Many of these disadvantages can be overcome by effective leadership of the team and by adoption of a number of methods of ensuring that a wide variety of views and opinions are introduced and considered. These range from encouragement of discussion with trusted associates outside the team to the assignment of certain members to study the other participants in detail and to be advocates of what is believed to be their points of view in all discussions.

Perhaps the greatest disadvantage of the task force approach is inherent in the temporary nature of the assignment of the members. After the first flush of interest in the task dies down, members may begin to look forward to the day when they can return to a more normal position in the organization. Anxieties may arise about future responsibilities or over real or imagined lost opportunities for advancement. A growing desire to wind up the assignment is, however, directly opposed to the need for a continuing treatment of most complex decision problems. This can be offset to some extent by a policy of rotating members through the team, but this in itself results in some loss of continuity.

The above disadvantages of the task force approach are often cited by those who favor consideration of all problems with which an organization is concerned within the normal framework of management. Consideration of any one problem by management in such a scheme is naturally only part-time, although it may be supported by full-time work by specialists in staff positions. The time devoted to the strategic consideration of a problem in such an arrangement is illustrated by the boxes in Figure 6.2. The interval between successive considerations of the same problem can be made shorter in cases of greater urgency and longer as such urgency subsides.

The treatment of complex problems as part of the normal work of management has the advantage that the widest range of knowledge and experience can be brought to bear on the problem. A second advantage is that the necessary continuing treatment of such problems is undertaken by a continuing function in the organization. Third, those involved in the decision making are those who must bear the responsibility for the outcomes. The main disadvantage of the approach is that managers and administrators at the higher level of organizations are often involved in a large number of different problems. Unless responsibility for work on some of these can be delegated, senior individuals may become overloaded and important problems may receive less attention than is necessary.

One means of overcoming these difficulties is to combine the management and task force approaches. This can be done by retaining responsibility for all complex problems that arise at a certain level in an organization in the managers and administrators at that level, but, at the same time, providing them with support in the form of a team dedicated full-time to this work. In this arrangement, the managers and administrators meet to consider a problem as often as the urgency of the matter requires. The team of full-time workers takes responsibility for all the continuing activities necessary in dealing with complex decision problems and prepares regular briefs on developments and on the results of analysis for the responsible managers. Decisions with regard to any necessary actions are made at the meetings between the team and the managers. The team of full-time personnel is often called a *policy analysis group.*

It is interesting to note that the interaction between a policy analysis group and management as envisaged above is similar to that which was originally advocated between senior managers and an operations research group.[1] Many of the authors of early works on operations research recommended the establishment of a group skilled in the techniques that would assist managers at the highest levels in an organization. A great deal has been achieved by such groups in recent years. Many large operational and administrative problems have been studied, with the result that substantial improvements in the efficiency of routine operations has been achieved.

The problems to which the quantitative techniques of operations research are applicable are not, however, those in which senior managers are most directly concerned. Large and repetitive operational and administrative problems are usually the responsibility of the middle and lower levels of management. Groups of specialists in operations research have, therefore, often found themselves engaged in problems that are not the immediate responsibility of those in the most senior echelons of management. Senior managers have come to regard specialist teams (especially those engaged in quantitative analysis) as important components of the organization, but not as potential contributors to the resolution of their most complex problems. A policy analysis group with members skilled in the nonquantitative methods described earlier in this text and which operates in conjunction with managers engaged in complex decision problems may well provide the element of support that many senior managers have found to be lacking in the past.

### ATTITUDES AND BEHAVIOR OF
### THOSE INVOLVED IN TREATMENT OF
### COMPLEX DECISION PROBLEMS

The attitudes and behavior of those involved in the treatment and resolution of complex decision problems often have significant effects on the results that are achieved. In some cases, the behavior of those involved is a direct result of frustration over the intractable nature of the problems they are dealing with. In other cases, the results are affected by the relationships between the individuals who are taking part in the resolution process.

One situation that is often encountered arises when several staff members have been named to a committee to conduct their organization's part in a problem situation. While they are assessing the situation and recommending courses of action, the members of the committee often consciously or unconsciously participate in an internal problem that is hierarchically subordinate to that being encountered by the organization as a whole. This subproblem is frequently concerned with promotion, with standing in the organization, or with the achievement of a reward (or the opposite), such as appointment to a particularly desirable (or undesirable) geographic area. The activities in the subproblem are often referred to nervously as "internal politics."

A small amount of activity in the subproblem is often beneficial to competent management and treatment of the larger situation. However, when the considerations of the subproblem become dominant in the minds of the personnel involved this can have major effects on the treatment of the problem being considered on behalf of the organization. Moves and actions applicable to the larger problem are often judged more on their effect in the subproblem than on their effectiveness in the area for which they were devised. Individuals and departments may support actions and initiatives only if they feel that some credit will accrue to them in the internal subproblem. Certain aspects of the larger problem may be regarded by all involved as too sensitive relative to the subproblem to be treated by the group at all. The tendency in such cases is for sensitive topics to be referred to more senior levels without appraisal or recommendations.

Members of an organization charged with resolving a complex decision problem sometimes express resignation about their ability to achieve a satisfactory resolution. This attitude is often linked to the high degree of uncertainty involved in the problem. It is sometimes thought preferable to take no action than to recognize the uncertainty and the need to work within the limitations that it imposes. In some cases, the feeling of despair regarding the ability to resolve a complex problem is enhanced by the fact that no quick solution is obtainable. Incremental measures do not seem to offer what will be regarded by others as a successful resolution. The fact that options have been kept open and that bad outcomes have been avoided is often thought to be too negative a result. Even if a degree of success is achieved, there is usually no satisfactory measure by which it can be assessed. There is often the feeling that a more desirable outcome would have been possible with a little more time or with a little more good fortune.

Those encountering complex decision problems in organizations sometimes give the impression that they prefer to work (at least some of the time) under conditions of urgency and pressure. There is exhilaration in a crisis and a sense of importance and accomplishment when an acceptable resolution is achieved in the face of deadlines and competition from others. The emphasis in the methods described earlier, however, is on steady and continuous work to avert crises and to down-play the aspect of confrontation. This is often less popular than the more heroic (and possibly more noticeable) activities involved in dealing with a crisis.

Another possible reason for dislike by senior managers and administrators for formal decision-making procedures is that these methods provide a structuring for (and therefore possibly an interference with) the process of decision making which is the senior decision makers' stock-in-trade. Senior members of organizations and communities are hired and paid on the basis of their prowess in dealing with complex decision problems. It may be difficult for even the most enlightened managers to admit that they need help in this task. There is often the suspicion that the methods and procedures proposed may usurp the responsibilities of senior managers in dealing with these problems. This is in no respect the case. The procedures outlined here are meant only as methods of structuring the treatment of complex decision problems. The major role in the resolution of these problems rests with the individuals involved, using judgements based on their accumulated knowledge and experience.

## SUPPORT REQUIRED FROM AN INFORMATION SYSTEM

In making these judgements, those involved in the resolution of complex decision problems require considerable support in gathering, processing, and presenting information relevant to the problem at hand. Methods of gathering such information related to a particular problem have been described in Chapter 3. It is desirable, however, to provide for the acquisition, classification, and storage of information of this nature as a continuing activity and as a complement to the special efforts directed toward solving a particular problem. The procedures involved in the continuing gathering, assessment, storage, and presentation of this information fall naturally into the area of the management information system.

Most existing management information systems are primarily concerned with quantitative data and, furthermore, with data of this nature that arise within the organization in which they operate. The greatest proportion of these data refer to the accounting and financial control functions. This is natural because these are important internal functions, and also because the data and information with which they are concerned are easily defined and well understood. The development of information systems has been concentrated on the collection, processing, storage, and presentation of quantitative data primarily because the need for this activity exists and because it is an area in which it is possible to achieve some success using existing knowledge and techniques.[2, 3]

Some of this quantitative data may be important to those involved in the resolution of complex decision problems. However, it is vital that a much broader range of information be available also. In a far-sighted article published in 1961, Daniel described this broader range of information as being of three basic types:[4]

1. *Environmental Information*—describing the social, political, and economic aspect of the climate in which a business (government or community) operates or may operate in the future;

2. *Competitive Information*—explaining the past performance and the programs and plans of competing companies (participants);

3. *Internal Information*—indicating a company's (participant's) own strengths and weaknesses.

Daniel's early description of the information required by managers requires only a small amount of modification and updating to correspond to a description of the required information concerning the participants as well as the social, technological, and natural elements of the environment in a complex decision problem.

Much of this information is of a different nature than the quantitative data that is the prime constituent of most existing information systems. This information required is usually in the form of opinions, assessments and judgements rather than of purely numerical data. It may be in the form of quotations from newspaper articles or other published and unpublished documents. The context and author of such quotations may also be important, so that it is often necessary to store and present considerable amounts of written material in order to convey the essence of the information. However, techniques for storage and retrieval of such material are readily available and the functions serviced by the information system are primarily concerned with providing efficient methods of indexing, search, and retrieval related to the documents and subjects in question.

In starting to build this new component of the information system, it is often difficult to determine the exact nature of the material that should be acquired and stored. Furthermore, it is sometimes difficult to obtain a concise statement from those involved in dealing with complex decision problems with regard to information that they need. Most managers and administrators in such situations feel the need for as much information as they can digest, mainly as a counter to the uncertainty inherent in the situation with which they are dealing. This suggests that the highest priority should be given to information that has the greatest effect in reducing uncertainty. If this prescription is too general, perhaps the best course is to gather and store all information pertinent to the participants and the various environmental elements of current complex decision problems and of those that are anticipated to arise in the future. This may represent a major increase in the data-gathering and processing activities of many organizations, but a step in this direction will provide valuable support to those engaged in dealing with problems of this nature.

## SUMMARY

The model of the process of resolution of complex decision problems discussed in the earlier chapters is broad and flexible. The associated methods and techniques are drawn from practical experience and a wide range of more technical considerations. Both the model and the methodology are likely to be readily understood by those involved in the resolution of complex decision problems. Furthermore, they take into account most of the major characteristics of those problems.

Although the model described is a likely basis for favorable resolution of complex decision problems, it is, at best, only a representation of the real process. It should not, therefore, be used to replace proven practical procedures, but rather to provide a structure and underpinning to the activities of those involved with such problems.

Many of the activities and procedures that have been described as desirable in the solution of complex decision problems are closely related to the conventional organizational activities of information gathering, policy making, and planning. However, those associated with communication, negotiation, and bargaining with other participants are often much less formalized in modern organizations.

The work of resolution of complex decision problems in an organization can be made the responsibility of a task force set up to deal with each problem as it occurs. This has the advantage of concentrating effort, of encouraging dynamic leadership, and of providing an atmosphere in which creative thought and innovation are possible. There are, however, disadvantages to the approach, ranging from the possibility of group-oriented thought to the problems that may arise from the temporary nature of the assignment for members of the team. Another approach often advocated is that in which the problems are dealt with by management in the normal course of its activities, supported as necessary by the work of those in staff positions. This method of working has the advantage of providing continuing treatment of problems and of bringing the widest possible range of judgement and experience to bear on them.

The management and task force approaches can be combined. Responsibility for resolution of complex decision problems is retained with management at the level at which they arise. Support is provided to those responsible for resolution in the form of a team of full-time personnel specializing in the treatment of complex problems. Such a team is sometimes called a *policy analysis group*. It bears a relationship to senior management similar to that once envisaged for operations research groups.

There are a number of factors that may detract from the effectiveness of organizational procedures for treating complex decision problems. Personnel involved in resolution of a problem may, for example, be more concerned with an internal (hierarchically subordinate) problem involving promotion or status within the organization. There is often a sense of despair regarding the possibility of finding an acceptable form of resolution because no quick and readily apparent solution is obtainable. Even if an acceptable outcome is achieved, it is often difficult to establish a measure by which the success of the work can be judged. Personnel often prefer to work in crisis conditions, whereas organizational procedures tend to stress continuous work to avert such conditions. Senior managers sometimes feel that procedures designed to structure and support the treatment of complex decision problems usurp, to some extent, the responsibilities for which they have been hired.

Data gathering is an area in which existing organizational procedures are often inadequate. The information required by those involved in dealing with complex decision problems is different in some respects from that which is provided by many existing information systems. Whereas the quantitative data provided by such systems may be an important part of the requirements of those dealing with complex decision problems, a considerable range of information is also required regarding the elements of the problem at hand. Much of this information is nonquantitative and much may be subjective. A separate component of the information system is usually required to provide this information.

## DISCUSSION TOPICS

1. Are models of the process of resolution of complex decision problems useful as a basis for establishing organizational procedures for dealing with them? What safeguards should be taken to ensure that factors not included in the models are not forgotten?
2. In what manner do you think resistance to the establishment of organizational procedures for dealing with complex decision problems might arise? How would you convince managers and administrators to accept such procedures?
3. Can policy making be regarded as essentially the work of dealing with complex decision problems?
4. How should planning relate to policy making and to the treatment of complex decision problems?
5. Is it true that communication with other participants in a complex decision problem is often neglected in modern organizations? If so, how could this deficiency be improved?
6. Would you establish a task force to deal with a particularly difficult problem or would you expect managers to deal with it in the course of their normal work? What advantages would you expect to accrue from the course you select?
7. Suppose that you were designated to establish a policy analysis group. What would you suggest as its terms of reference? What type of persons would you choose to staff it?
8. How could you ensure that the policy analysis group provided real service to senior managers and administrators?

9. How can you prevent a problem internal to a group dealing with a complex decision problem from having undesirable effects on the larger problem in which they are engaged?
10. Is it true that most existing information systems are of limited help to those engaged in the resolution of complex decision problems? If so, why is this? If not, provide a description of the manner in which such systems are of practical use in these circumstances.
11. Can the designer of a management information system expect to receive detailed guidance from managers and administrators regarding the information they need in the resolution of a complex decision problem? If not, how can a knowledge of these requirements be obtained?
12. What techniques would you suggest for storage of information contained in documents? How would you index this information for easy reference?

#### REFERENCES

1. Morse, P. M., and G. E. Kimball. *Methods of Operations Research,* 1st rev. ed. Cambridge, Mass.: Technology Press, M.I.T., 1951.
2. Radford, K. J. "Information Systems and Managerial Decision Making." *OMEGA,* The International Journal of Management Science 2, 1974.
3. Radford, K. J. *Information Systems in Management.* Reston, Va.: Reston Publishing Co. Inc., 1973.
4. Daniel, D. R. "Management Information Crisis." *Harvard Business Review,* Sept.-Oct. 1961, pp. 91–101.

# Glossary

**accommodative move**—a bargaining move designed to bring about an atmosphere conducive to settlement of a conflict.

**action space**—the arena in which the interactions among the participants in a complex decision problem and between them and the environment of the problem take place.

**analysis of options**—a practical method (derived from metagame theory) for investigating the strategic structure of a complex problem.

**assurance**—a bargaining tactic designed to maintain the element of challenge inherent in the different preferences of the participants for outcomes in a conflict situation but which does so in a manner that minimizes the possibility that the challenge will be considered to be intimidating.

**bounded rationality**—a description of a type of decision making behavior under conditions of uncertainty in which a satisfactory rather than an optimum alternative is selected (see satisficing).

**coercive move**—a bargaining move designed to influence opponents to accept one's more preferred outcomes.

**completely specified decision problem**—a decision problem the characteristics of which are completely known (or agreed by those involved) so that rational solution is possible by standard techniques (also called a "programmed" decision).

**complex decision problem**—a decision problem that cannot be completely specified and that typically involves uncertainty, multiple objectives, and more than one participant.

**conflict point**—a situation sometimes reached in bargaining in which all (or most) participants are not moving towards a settlement.

**cross impact analysis**—a method of estimating the possible effect of the occurrence or nonoccurrence of one event on the occurrence or nonoccurrence of another.

**Delphi**—a method of gathering qualitative data involving a succession of questionnaires in which responses to earlier questions are used in formulating later inquiries.

**elements of the environment**—social, technological, and natural factors that constitute the characteristics of the environment of a complex decision problem.

**environment**—the action space of a complex decision problem.

**equilibrium**—a possible outcome of a complex decision problem, from which it is not to the advantage of any participant to move, provided that the others do not.

**fractionating**—a method proposed for dealing with conflict in which the main issue is divided into lesser components that are dealt with separately and in sequence.

**guaranteed improvement** a unilateral move from a scenario by a participant that would give him a preferred outcome no matter what the other participants do (in the analysis of options).

**incrementalism**—a strategy of decision making in which only incremental steps are considered, in which the results of actions are reviewed continually, and in which new actions are decided after such reviews.

**information set**—the information available to a participant in a complex decision problem, consisting of that derived from past experience and that gathered in relation to the actual problem.

**issue machine**—an overall model of the process of consideration of a complex decision problem. A number of alternative solutions are considered at a number of stations (participants) and in each case, the suitability of each alternative as a solution to the problem is reviewed. Consideration may continue over a number of rounds. An alternative chosen in each of a number of successive rounds is regarded as a stable outcome.

**linkages**—links between concurrent problems, both in the *horizontal* sense of problems of roughly equal status and in the *vertical* and hierarchical sense.

**log-rolling**—a term describing an agreement between two participants in which one supports the other in one problem in return for similar support in another.

**membership**—a term describing the relationship between participants in a complex decision problem and emphasizing their common interest in maintaining the relationship.

**metaequilibrium**—an equilibrium that could come about by mutual agreement between participants in a conflict situation as a result of their mutual knowledge of each others' intentions.

**metagame**—a hypothetical situation that would arise in a conflict situation if one participant knew the choices of options of all the others involved—the basic theory behind the analysis of options.

**mixed scanning**—a method of data gathering and decision making in which consideration is given to matters at a series of levels in rotation rather than concentrating on only one level.

**Nature**—a pseudoparticipant in the analysis of options to which is attributed (as options) all natural and quasi-natural events.

**outcome**—a future scenario that could be brought about by joint actions by the participants in a complex decision problem.

**P-stability**—a situation in which the same reasons count with the same weight for or against the alternatives in a decision problem, regardless of which stations (in the issue-machine sense) act in which sequence in each successive round, and the same policy is adopted as the output of the process after each round.

**participant**—an individual, group, or organization that has the power to influence the outcome of a complex decision problem.

**perception**—the understanding of a participant of the complex problem in which he is engaged.

**power**—the ability to impose an outcome on other participants in a complex decision problem (defined in the relative rather than the absolute sense).

**pure communication move**—a move in bargaining involving only passage of information.

**quasi-natural event**—an event caused by the action of unknown people that, for want of better explanation, is often assumed to be natural—the unintended consequences of others' intended actions.

**risk**—a term used in describing bargaining situations to denote the possibility of a bad outcome.

**sanction**—a joint action by some participants to prevent one or more others from attaining a more preferred outcome (in the analysis of options).

**satisficing**—choosing an alternative that is good enough rather than optimal.

**scenario**—a description of a present or future situation in terms of participants and their available options.

**sensitivity testing**—a testing of the sensitivity of the results of an analysis to changes in the basic assumptions.

**stability**—an outcome of a conflict situation that can be achieved by the participants proceeding to a metaequilibrium and remaining there.

**strategic structure**—the result of analysis of the interaction of the preferences for outcomes of the participants in a complex decision problem.

**structural move**—a bargaining move that involves the narrowing or widening of the options of a participant usually by committing assets or resources.

**technological forecasting**—a term covering methods of estimating future values of parameters on the basis of past data.

**time-dependency**—a term describing possible changes with time of such elements of a complex decision problem as the participants, their options, their preferences, and the elements of the environment.

**uncertainty**—a state arising from possession of only limited amounts of information concerning a problem.

**uncertainty avoidance**—methods of reducing the effects of uncertainty on the outcome of decisions.

**unilateral improvement**—an improvement from a particular scenario that can be achieved by a participant acting unilaterally, but that might be subject to sanctions by the other participants (in the analysis of options).

**value system**—patterns of belief of participants or of societies that govern behavior in choosing between alternatives and are also the basis for standards of conduct.

# Index